SIMPLY BISHOP'S

SIMPLY

JOHN BISHOP

BISHOP'S

EASY SEASONAL RECIPES

Douglas & McIntyre

VANCOUVER/TORONTO

Dedicated to the memory of Dr. Michael Smith, a man who liked

his food and wine and who also liked things to be rather simple

Douglas & McIntyre
2323 Quebec Street, Suite 201
Vancouver, British Columbia
Canada V5T 4S7
www.douglas-mcintyre.com

Editing by Saeko Usukawa
Cover and interior design by Peter Cocking
Photography by John Sherlock
Printed and bound in Canada by Friesens
Printed on acid-free paper

We gratefully acknowledge the financial support
of the Canada Council for the Arts, the British
Columbia Arts Council, the Province of British
Columbia through the Book Publishing Tax
Credit and the Government of Canada through
the Book Publishing Industry Development
Program (BPIDP) for our publishing activities.

Library and Archives Canada
Cataloguing in Publication
Bishop, John, 1944–
    Simply Bishop's
    Includes index.
    ISBN 978-1-55054-949-2 (bound)
    ISBN 978-1-55365-388-2 (paper)

    1. Cookery, Canadian—British Columbia
style. 2. Cookery—British Columbia—
Vancouver. 3. Bishop's (Restaurant) I. Green,
Dennis, 1969– II. Title.
TX945.5.B58B582 2002   641.5′09711′33
C2002-910688-5

Contents

"SIMPLE" AND "SEASONAL" are the two words that I would use to describe the recipes in and the inspiration for this cookbook. Simplicity has always been one of the qualities that we aim for at Bishop's Restaurant: simplicity and casual elegance. But "simple" is sometimes difficult to achieve. It's hard, for example, to learn to leave well enough alone, to let wonderfully fresh ingredients speak for themselves and not to smother them by doing too much.

A few years ago, Dennis Green, chef at Bishop's Restaurant, and I had the idea of starting cooking classes because we wanted to show people that cooking good food can be a pleasure. It can even be therapeutic to work with your hands and get in touch with your senses. I love to put on some good jazz, pour a glass of wine and forget my cares by entering the world of the kitchen.

In the course of creating recipes for those cooking classes, Dennis and I began to simplify the preparation part—but without sacrificing our love of combining flavours, textures and colours. At the same time, we were beginning to realize that organically grown and raised food really does have better flavour, and we have developed relationships with local suppliers, many of whom follow the organic way, like the King family at Hazelmere Farm and Milan Djordvich at Stoney Paradise Farm. That led, naturally enough, to the fact that vegetables, fruits, herbs, seafood and many other foods ripen or are at their best at different seasons throughout the year. Above all, we must keep in mind that the meals we put on the table are only as good as the ingredients used to make them, and both professional chefs and home cooks are starting to look more closely and at the food we are serving. Quality and freshness are the most important factors in good ingredients, but equally as exciting is the fact that now we are also getting to know the people who grow our vegetables, fruit and herbs, and who supply our seafood and meat. To quote a well known farmer friend of mine, Michael Abelman, "We are putting a face to our food."

Each season offers its own delights. Spring is a time of reawakening and rebirth and the promise of good things to come. It also brings back fond memories of my childhood, eating lots of homemade lemon pancakes on Shrove Tuesday—we often forget that spring is the real season for citrus fruits. I look forward to morel mushrooms, local asparagus, fiddlehead ferns, young salad greens, halibut and spring salmon, tender spring lamb. Rhubarb, with its refreshing tartness and beautiful pink colour, seems to sum up spring.

Summer is a gloriously bountiful season, with an amazing parade of vegetables, fruits and berries ripening week by week. Summer is the time to dust off the barbecue and cook a thick fillet of wild sockeye or to go on picnics. It's the time for cold fruit soups, crisp salads and vegetables bursting with flavour: lush field-grown lettuces, vine-ripened heirloom tomatoes, sweet juicy peppers, purple and white baby eggplants, green and yellow snap beans. Summer always reminds me of these words written on a small plaque, which I read as a young child whilst seated on my grandmother's outside loo: *The kiss of the sun for pardon / The songs of the birds for mirth / You are closest to God's heart in a garden / Than anywhere else on Earth.*

Autumn is the time of year to go for long drives through the countryside to marvel at the fall colours and to visit roadside stands that display the rich end-of-summer harvest. Piles of orange pumpkins, strings of decorative ears of maize, braids of garlic, baskets of nuts, fantastically shaped squashes and gourds, red and green pyramids of ripe apples and pears. Different mushrooms are also in season, such as chanterelles, porcinis and matsutake. The days are getting shorter and cooler, so it's a perfect time to change culinary gears to a heartier kind of cooking that includes soups, game, braised meats and seafood stews.

Winter brings colder weather. It's a time to stay close to home and hearth, to slow down and savour comfort food. The gardens and fields are no longer as colourful, but there is still much to discover out there. Earthy tasting beets make a great winter salad or a soul-warming soup. I love to serve crunchy salads using cabbages and fennel, braised winter organic greens like ruby chard and curly kale, saffron-coloured seafood broth, roasts that have been slow-cooked for hours with root vegetables, sweet rich desserts.

Now it's time for you to get cooking with these simpler recipes and great seasonal ingredients. Remember to take the time to feast your eyes on the beautiful colours and shapes, to take pleasure in the chopping and stirring, to breathe in the aromas and, above all, to enjoy cooking.

ONE SECRET TO ENTERTAINING, as you've probably guessed, is to keep it simple. Another secret is to plan. A third secret is to prepare dishes or parts of dishes ahead of time as much as you can.

Now that you want to host a dinner party, the first decision is: will it be a sit-down dinner or a buffet meal? Next, if there isn't already a reason such as a birthday, think of a theme, as this will help in planning the menu, setting the table and choosing wines. (See page 7 for some seasonal menu suggestions for special occasions.)

I also like the idea of asking someone to give a brief reading (no more than a few minutes long) before the meal, perhaps an amusing short story about food or a favourite poem. Always remember to celebrate the moment, no matter how big, no matter how small.

GETTING READY

Find out if any of your guests have food allergies, if they eat meat or not, if they eat seafood or not. Figure out a menu, trying to use fresh local seasonal ingredients and dishes that you are confident about cooking. For a sit-down dinner, choose a starter (such as soup or salad) and a dessert that can be made ahead. This will free you up to concentrate on the main course, to spend time with your guests and to enjoy yourself.

Once you've settled on the menu, be sure to read the recipes carefully from beginning to end. Write out a shopping list and then look for the freshest ingredients. If you're going to be using ingredients whose state can't be predicted, like avocados, buy one or two extra ones just in case. Remember to put flowers on your shopping list, as a few bouquets always add to the sense of occasion and festivity with their colour and scent.

Set the table well ahead of time, even before you start kitchen preparations. Handwritten or printed menus add a nice touch, and so do place cards. Small gifts in keeping with the theme are a good ice-breaker, and they don't have to be expensive.

IN THE KITCHEN

Make an order-of-work list so that you know what you'll have to do and when in the kitchen. Once you're ready to start cooking, gather together and set out all the ingredients, utensils and cookware you will need. I've learned over the years that it's best to clean and put away cookware and utensils as soon as I'm finished with them, to keep the kitchen tidy and organized as I prepare other dishes.

Prepare ahead by prescooping palate cleansers such as water ices or sorbet, or ice cream desserts, into balls, and keep them frozen on a tray in the freezer so that you can serve them more easily. For dessert, you have a wide choice of ones that can be made ahead. But if your dessert is to be baked and served hot, make sure that the oven is preheated at the correct temperature well ahead of time. If a recipe calls for whipped cream, you can whip it ahead of time and store it covered in the refrigerator.

Always try to serve cold food on chilled (not frozen) plates, and to serve warm food on warmed plates. (If you run out of room on or in your stove, you can warm plates in your dishwasher.) The best way to keep food and sauces hot is to set a roasting or lasagna-type deep-sided metal pan on the stove top; half fill the pan with warm water on a low-heat burner. Into this water bath, place metal or ceramic containers of sauces, cooked veggies and even mashed potatoes, lightly covered with aluminum foil. This is a simple way to keep food nice and warm, without burning.

When it comes to plating the various courses, the most efficient way is to set out all the dishes for a course and do them assembly-line style. When presenting the main course, the safe route is to plate only the meat or fish, along with any sauce; serve everything else on the side on warmed platters or bowls in the centre of the table. Some desserts can also be served at the table.

At the end of the meal, just do the very essential clean up, as there is nothing worse than a fine meal followed by hours of work. Good crystal wine glasses should be rinsed and left to drip-dry on towels; don't try to clean and polish them after dinner, as more glasses are broken and hands are cut this way. Leave them until the morning. There shouldn't be many pots and pans and other utensils if you've cleaned up along the way; any that are left can be put to soak in the sink. Fill up the dishwasher, of course, and that's it.

BUFFETS

For a buffet, the ideal type of foods are easy-to-"self serve" dishes, such as a pre-carved roast or chops, and those that can easily be portioned, such as chicken or salmon. A variety of salads is always appealing; green salads should have the dressing served on the side, otherwise the salads will become limp.

What I love about creating a home buffet table for a party is that you can do as little or as much as you want. You can set it up inside or outdoors, depending on the season. Two tables are best. Use a small table for plates, napkins, cutlery, wine and soft drinks; arrange the food on a large table. To make the main buffet table look more attractive and interesting, create a multi-level effect by placing a few small boxes of different heights on top of it. To finish it off, give the buffet a unified look by covering the boxes and table with two or three tablecloths. On top of the boxes, display a candelabra or a vase of flowers or a platter of food. For more visual appeal, place a decorative bottle of olive oil beside a basket of bread-sticks and a variety of hearty breads. Use platters for meat or fish, and ceramic, glass or wooden bowls for salads or desserts, and be sure to put out lots of tongs and big spoons for serving.

Food safety is important, particularly when food is left out at room temperature for even a short period of time. If the buffet is outside, make sure it is protected from the sun with a large patio umbrella. I always keep seafood dishes cold on trays of crushed ice. Meat or fish that is served hot must be kept hot.

BEVERAGES

For a buffet dinner, I usually like to offer a choice of one white wine and one red wine, as well as an assortment of soft drinks and mineral water, so that people can help themselves to what they want. Riesling and Gewürztraminer are popular and go well with seafood. With chicken or dishes that have cream-based sauces, serve a bigger, richer style of white wine, such as a Pinot Gris, Chardonnay or Viognier. Red meat dishes seem to demand more robust red wines. A simple guideline is to try to pair up the ingredients and their country of origin with a wine from the same country (although nothing is set in stone, and you should simply drink the wines you enjoy). For example, tomatoes and peppers indicate that the recipe may have originated from a southern climate, so I would try choose a wine from those areas, such as France's Rhône Valley, southern Italy or Spain. Less robust food flavours suggest a more northern style, lighter red wine, such as a Pinot Noir, Merlot or Cabernet Sauvignon. All of the entrée recipes in this cookbook have suggestions for the wine to serve with them.

Recently, a friend of mine told me how much she enjoys entertaining and that she keeps a special book to record these events. She makes note of the date of the dinner, the names of the people who attended, the menu, and any special food needs such as allergies. She also notes any variation and changes she has made to recipes, what worked and what didn't, what people liked and what they didn't. I am afraid that I'm not this organized, but I do occasionally keep records of very special functions that I have hosted. A cooking/entertaining journal is not only handy but a keepsake of special events in your life.

A VERY SPRING BRUNCH

Herb Crepes with Hand-peeled
Shrimp and Smoked Salmon *14*

Roasted Spring Salmon with
Rhubarb Compote *76*

Grilled Asparagus Spears with
Raspberry-Shallot Vinaigrette *115*

Lemon-Orange Pound Cake with
Grand Marnier Syrup *144*

A GLORIOUS SUMMER BARBECUE

Honey-Lime Scallop Brochettes *20*

Heirloom Tomato and Sweet Onion
Salad with Balsamic Syrup and
Basil Oil *64*

Thick-cut Spice-rubbed Steak
with Red Wine Sauce and
Roasted Fingerling Potatoes *90*

Gooseberry and Almond Crumble *146*

A THANKSGIVING FEAST

Warm Chanterelle Tart with
Green Peppercorns *21*

Autumn Greens with
Raspberry Vinaigrette and
Toasted Pumpkin Seeds *67*

Roast Turkey Breast with
Port-Cranberry Compote *99*

Roasted Butternut Squash with
Maple-Thyme Butter *128*

Sweet Potato and Celery Root Purée *126*

Spiced Poached Pears with
Red Wine Caramel *150*

A NEW YEAR'S EVE BUFFET

Oysters on the Half Shell with
Apple Cider–Shallot Vinaigrette and
Other Garnishes *31*

Beet Salad with Raspberry Vinaigrette
and Goat Cheese *69*

Grilled Prawns with
Pumpkin Risotto *110*

Slow-cooked Pork Shoulder with
Pan-roasted Vegetables *105*

Chèvre Cheesecake with Dried Fruits
and Apricot Brandy Syrup *160*

APPETIZERS

AUTUMN

Warm Chanterelle Tart with
Green Peppercorns *21*

Oyster Stew with Leeks and
White Vermouth *22*

Tea-smoked Duck Breast
with Shiitake Mushrooms and
Green Tea Vinaigrette *24*

Roasted Pear and Goat Cheese
Phyllo Pastries *27*

WINTER

Chicken Liver and Green Peppercorn
Pâté with Herb Toast *28*

Oysters on the Half Shell with
Apple Cider–Shallot Vinaigrette
and Other Garnishes *31*

Scallops in Rice Paper with
Sesame-Ginger Dressing *32*

Potted Shrimp Infused with
Savoury Herbs and Garlic *33*

SPRING

Sake-and-Ginger Steamed Clams *10*

Fresh Morel Mushrooms with
Asparagus Tips *11*

Asian Tuna Tartare with
Scallion Pancakes *12*

Herb Crepes with Hand-peeled Shrimp
and Smoked Salmon *14*

SUMMER

Warm Tomato and Asiago Tart
with Red Onion *16*

Smoked Salmon and Cucumber
with Pickled Ginger *17*

Walnut-crusted Goat Cheese
with Red Pepper Coulis *19*

Honey-Lime Scallop Brochettes *20*

Sake-and-Ginger Steamed Clams

2 lb.	fresh clams in the shell	1 kg
1 Tbsp.	butter	30 mL
1	garlic clove, chopped	1
1	shallot, finely minced	1
1 Tbsp.	chopped fresh ginger	15 mL
1 Tbsp.	chopped fresh cilantro	15 mL
1 cup	dry sake	250 mL
	Salt and freshly ground black pepper	

4 servings

The idea of cooking fresh clams in something other than the traditional white wine came from a chat with Michael, who works at the Lobster Man store where we get a lot of our seafood. He was excited about a clam dish that he had cooked the previous evening, and of course this piqued my interest. He even suggested using vodka as an alternative to white wine, but I prefer sake. Here is my version—I think you will enjoy the difference in taste. Try to get the smaller manila clams, because they are so tender and sweet.

You won't need to clean the clams, as those sold commercially usually have been "purged," so that any sand in them has been flushed out prior to going to market.

TO MAKE Tap any clams whose shells are open; discard those that do not close.

Melt butter in a soup pot on medium-high heat. Sauté garlic, shallot, ginger and cilantro for 2 to 3 minutes. Add clams and pour in sake. Season lightly with salt and pepper.

Cover the pot tightly and steam clams just until their shells open, about 5 minutes. Discard any whose shells remain closed.

Steamed clams cooked this way can be served hot or cold. I prefer them fresh and hot right out of their shells.

Fresh Morel Mushrooms with Asparagus Tips

It's a sure sign of spring when these delicious morsels start showing up at the market. Morels are very often dried to preserve them and so are available year round, but I really enjoy fresh ones cooked and served this way, with either green or the very special white asparagus. When shopping for mushrooms and asparagus, one way to check both of them for freshness is to make sure that the stem bottoms are nice and moist.

TO MAKE Cut off and discard stems of mushrooms. If mushrooms are small, leave them whole. If they are large, cut in half.

Melt butter in a frying pan on medium-high heat. Sauté mushrooms and shallot until tender, 3 to 4 minutes.

Deglaze the pan by adding white wine and chicken stock, stirring to loosen the browned bits on the bottom. Stir in whipping cream. Turn down the heat to medium and cook, uncovered, until sauce has reduced and thickened, about 15 minutes. Season to taste with salt and pepper. Keep warm on low heat while you cook asparagus.

Bring a small pot of salted water to a boil. While water is heating, cut off and discard bottoms of asparagus so that the spears are 2 to 3 inches/5 to 7.5 cm long. Plunge asparagus into the boiling water and cook until tender, 3 to 4 minutes. Drain.

To serve, place mushrooms on warmed plates, making sure each has equal amounts of sauce and mushrooms. Arrange 4 asparagus spears on each plate. Drizzle truffle oil over everything.

8 oz.	fresh morel mushrooms	250 g
1 Tbsp.	butter	15 mL
1	shallot, sliced	1
½ cup	dry white wine	125 mL
½ cup	chicken stock	125 mL
½ cup	whipping cream	125 mL
	Salt and freshly ground black pepper	
16	asparagus spears	16
2 tsp.	truffle oil	10 mL

4 servings

Asian Tuna Tartare with Scallion Pancakes

¾ cup	flour	175 mL
¼ cup	rice flour	60 mL
2 tsp.	baking powder	10 mL
½ tsp.	salt	2.5 mL
	Pinch of freshly ground black pepper	
4	green onions, minced	4
1 Tbsp.	chopped fresh cilantro	15 mL
2	eggs	2
½ cup	water	125 mL
¼ cup	sesame oil	60 mL
1 tsp.	vegetable oil	5 mL

TUNA TARTARE

8 oz.	Ahi tuna	250 g
1	bunch fresh cilantro, finely chopped	1
4	sprigs fresh mint, finely chopped	4
½ tsp.	sambal oelek	2.5 mL
1 tsp.	grated fresh ginger	5 mL
2 Tbsp.	liquid honey	30 mL
1 Tbsp.	lime juice	15 mL
1 Tbsp.	fish sauce	15 mL
1 Tbsp.	soy sauce	15 mL
1 Tbsp.	mirin	15 mL
	Salad greens	
1 Tbsp.	toasted sesame seeds	15 mL

4 servings

This Asian version of tuna tartare is a big hit when served in smaller portions as part of an hors d'oeuvre platter. The scallion pancakes can be made ahead of time. If there are any extra ones, place them between sheets of wax paper in a plastic bag and freeze for later use.

TO MAKE PANCAKES Combine flour, rice flour, baking powder, salt, pepper, green onions and cilantro in a bowl.

In another bowl, whisk together eggs, water and sesame oil. Stir into flour mixture. Let batter rest for 15 minutes.

Heat vegetable oil in a nonstick frying or crepe pan on medium-high heat. Once the pan is hot, discard the oil and wipe out the pan gently with a paper towel. Spoon 1 Tbsp./15 mL batter into the pan and cook until golden, 1 to 2 minutes, then turn over and cook the other side. Repeat until batter is used up. Makes about 16 pancakes.

TUNA TARTARE Cut tuna into ⅛-inch/3-mm dice and refrigerate until needed.

Make marinade by combining cilantro, mint, sambal oelek, ginger, honey, lime juice, fish sauce, soy sauce and mirin. Toss marinade with tuna and allow to marinate for 10 minutes or so. (Do not add marinade to tuna more than half an hour ahead, as the fish can become discoloured from the marinade.)

To serve, place some salad greens on each chilled plate. On top of each serving of greens, place a 2 oz./60-mL ring mold (or medium cookie cutter) and spoon a quarter of the tuna mixture into it. Remove the molds and place 3 or 4 pancakes on the side of each plate. Garnish tuna with toasted sesame seeds.

Asian tuna tartare with scallion pancakes >

Herb Crepes with Hand-peeled Shrimp and Smoked Salmon

CREPES

½ cup	flour	125 mL
2 tsp.	chopped fresh chives	10 mL
2 tsp.	chopped fresh parsley	10 mL
	Salt and freshly ground black pepper	
¾ cup	milk	175 mL
1	egg	1
1 Tbsp.	butter, melted	15 mL
1 tsp.	vegetable oil	5 mL

FILLING

¼ cup	cream cheese	60 mL
½	lime, zest and juice	½
½	orange, zest and juice	½
4 oz.	smoked salmon, sliced	120 g
4 oz.	fresh hand-peeled shrimp	120 g

4 servings

This sushi-like dish can be served as an appetizer or an hors d'oeuvre. Best of all, it can be made a few hours ahead and kept refrigerated; in fact, it is better to make this dish 2 to 3 hours ahead because the extra time spent refrigerated helps to firm up the filling and makes slicing easier. The filled crepes can be stored for a day in the refrigerator. Try alternate fillings such as fresh crabmeat, lobster or even vegetables.

When it comes to serving, I like to garnish the rolled crepes with just a few spring greens, such as baby spinach leaves that have been lightly tossed with a small amount of oil-and-vinegar dressing.

TO MAKE CREPES Combine flour, chives and parsley in a bowl. Season with salt and pepper.

In another bowl, whisk together milk, egg and melted butter. Add to flour mixture. Mix well and allow batter to rest for 1 hour before using.

Heat vegetable oil in a nonstick 10-inch/25-cm frying or crepe pan on medium-high heat. Once the pan is hot, discard the oil and wipe out the pan gently with a paper towel. Spoon about ¼ cup/60 mL batter into the pan and swirl it around so that it coats the bottom evenly. Cook until crepe is dry around the edges and lightly coloured on the bottom, 1 to 2 minutes. Turn it over and cook until lightly browned on the other side, 1 to 2 minutes. Make 4 crepes. Allow to cool.

FILLING Combine cream cheese, zest and juice of lime and orange in a bowl. Mix well.

TO ASSEMBLE Spread crepes with cream cheese mixture. Arrange a quarter of the smoked salmon slices in a row, horizontally, along the middle of each crepe. Place a quarter of the shrimp in a row along the edge of the smoked salmon closest to you. Fold the bottom edge of the crepe over the shrimp and smoked salmon, then roll up tightly. Repeat for the other 3 crepes. Cover each crepe in plastic wrap and refrigerate until needed.

To serve as an appetizer, cut each rolled crepe in half on an angle and arrange on a plate.

To serve as an hors d'oeuvre, cut into slices 1 inch (2.5 cm) thick and arrange on a platter.

Warm Tomato and Asiago Tart with Red Onion

8 oz.	frozen puff pastry, thawed	250 g
1	small red onion	1
4	Roma (plum) tomatoes	4
1 Tbsp.	olive oil	15 mL
1 Tbsp.	chopped fresh basil	15 mL
½ cup	grated Asiago cheese	125 mL
	Olive oil for drizzling	
	Freshly ground black pepper	
	Fresh basil leaves for garnish	

4 tarts, each 4 inches/10 cm square

Ripe tomatoes, tangy Italian cheese and crunchy onions make this warm appetizer a very appealing alternative to salad. It's also ideal for a light summer lunch, with perhaps a cool glass of Pinot Gris, served outside under a umbrella,. For this recipe, I prefer to use Roma (also called plum) tomatoes, as they are drier and have a thicker skin than other varieties, so they hold up better when baked.

TO MAKE Preheat the oven to 400°F/200°C and line a baking sheet with parchment paper.

On a lightly floured surface, roll out puff pastry to form an 8-inch/20-cm square, ⅛ inch/3 mm thick. Cut into four 4-inch/10-cm squares. Prick pastry all over with a fork and refrigerate for 20 minutes.

Peel onion and slice as thinly as possible. Cut tomatoes into slices ¼ inch/6 mm thick.

Brush pastry squares with olive oil and sprinkle with chopped basil. Arrange tomato slices in a layer. Place a layer of onion slices over tomatoes and top with grated Asiago cheese. Drizzle with a little olive oil and sprinkle with a grinding of black pepper.

Place on the prepared baking sheet and bake until pastry is puffed and golden, about 15 minutes.

To serve, place each tart on a warmed plate and garnish with a couple of basil leaves.

Smoked Salmon and English Cucumber with Pickled Ginger

The pickled ginger and rice vinegar for this recipe are available at Japanese or Asian specialty food stores. While I'm there, I also like to pick up a small bunch of daikon sprouts to use for garnishing the plates.

TO MAKE Cut pickled ginger into thin strips.

Score the peel of cucumber along its length with the tines of a dinner fork to create a decorative stripe pattern. Cut into thin slices and set aside in a bowl.

In another bowl, combine pickled ginger and rice vinegar, then pour over cucumber. Cover and allow to marinate in the refrigerator for 30 minutes before serving.

To serve, place a circle of cucumber slices on each chilled salad plate, along with a puddle of rice vinegar from the marinade. Bunch up each salmon slice to form a rosette, then place three of them on the centre of each plate. Fill the centre of each salmon rosette with strips of pickled ginger from the marinade.

1 Tbsp.	pickled ginger, drained	15 mL
½	English cucumber	½
½ cup	rice vinegar	125 mL
6 oz.	smoked salmon (12 thin slices)	170 g

4 servings

Walnut-crusted Goat Cheese with Red Pepper Coulis

Goat cheese is very popular, especially served like this as a warm appetizer. The goat cheese we like to use in the restaurant is soft and creamy, and it comes from a talented farmer named David Wood, whose name has become synonymous with the art of cheese-making. His farm is located on British Columbia's beautiful Salt Spring Island.

TO MAKE COULIS Seed red pepper and cut into thin slices.

Place red wine vinegar and sugar in a small saucepan with a tight-fitting lid. Bring to a boil on medium-high heat, then add red pepper and shallot. Turn down the heat to low, cover, and simmer until vegetables soften, about 30 minutes. Remove from the stove and cool for 15 minutes.

Purée in a blender or food processor until smooth. Strain and refrigerate until needed.

GOAT CHEESE Divide goat cheese into 4 portions. Form each piece into a small patty about 2½ inches/6 cm in diameter. Chill thoroughly in the refrigerator.

Place bread crumbs and walnuts in a blender or food processor and finely chop.

Roll each cheese piece in flour, then dip in beaten egg, and cover with bread crumb mixture.

Heat olive oil in a frying pan on medium heat. Fry breaded cheese pieces until golden all over and heated through, 2 to 3 minutes. Drain on paper towels.

Pour 2 Tbsp./30 mL red pepper coulis to form a small pool on each plate, then place a piece of breaded cheese in the centre. Garnish with a few sprigs of arugula or other baby spring salad greens.

< Walnut-crusted goat cheese
  with red pepper coulis

COULIS

1	red pepper	1
½ cup	red wine vinegar	125 mL
¼ cup	sugar	60 mL
1	shallot, sliced	1

GOAT CHEESE

8 oz.	soft goat cheese	250 g
½ cup	dry bread crumbs	125 mL
½ cup	walnuts	125 mL
	Flour for breading	
1	egg, beaten lightly	1
¼ cup	olive oil	60 mL
	Arugula or baby spring salad greens for garnish	

4 servings

Honey-Lime Scallop Brochettes

16	large scallops (1 lb./500 g)	16
1 Tbsp.	fresh lime juice	15 mL
1 tsp.	liquid or melted honey	5 mL
1 Tbsp.	sesame oil	15 mL
	Salt and freshly ground black pepper	
	Vegetable oil	
2	limes cut in half	2
2 Tbsp.	chopped fresh cilantro	30 mL

4 servings

Cooking on brochettes (skewers) is an ideal way to quickly grill these delicate seafood morsels, and you won't have to spend time painstakingly flipping each individual scallop. The brochettes can be cooked either on a barbecue or in a small grill pan on top of the stove.

TO MAKE Soak 8 bamboo skewers in water for 30 minutes so they won't burn. Use 2 parallel skewers for each brochette, so the scallops won't move and are easy to turn. Thread 4 scallops on each pair of skewers and place in a flat dish.

Combine lime juice, honey and sesame oil in a bowl. Drizzle over scallops. Cover and allow to marinate for 30 minutes in the refrigerator.

Preheat the barbecue or grill pan on high heat, then wipe the grill rack or pan quickly with a vegetable oil–soaked paper towel or rag to help prevent sticking.

Grill brochettes until just cooked, 3 to 4 minutes per side. Grill limes at the same time, cut side down, for 3 to 4 minutes.

To serve, remove scallops from skewers and arrange on a warmed platter (or simply place brochettes on a platter) and sprinkle with chopped cilantro. Garnish with grilled lime halves.

Warm Chanterelle Tart with Green Peppercorns

Chanterelles are little golden trumpet-shaped mushrooms. When freshly picked, they smell woodsy and have a delicate flavour. They have become a fall favourite at the restaurant, lightly cooked and spiced with these fiery Madagascar green peppercorns, which come packed in brine and are available in specialty markets and food shops. As a substitute for the Madagascar peppercorns, you can use a smaller amount of pink peppercorns.

TO MAKE PASTRY Preheat the oven to 375°F/190°C.

Combine flour, cornmeal and salt in a bowl and mix well. Cut butter into small pieces, then combine with flour mixture until texture is mealy. Add water and mix thoroughly. Cover with plastic wrap and allow to rest for 30 minutes.

Roll out dough on a lightly floured surface to a thickness of ⅛ inch/3 mm. Cut into four rounds, each 5 inches/ 13 cm in diameter, and fit them into 4-inch/10-cm tart pans (or 4 spaces in a muffin tin). Prick bottoms of pastry and bake until golden brown, 15 to 20 minutes.

FILLING Melt butter in a saucepan on medium heat. Sauté shallots, garlic and mushrooms until tender, 2 to 3 minutes.

Deglaze the pan by adding sherry and stirring to loosen the browned bits on the bottom. Add chicken stock, green (or pink) peppercorns and thyme. Bring to a boil on medium-high heat and simmer, uncovered, until almost all of the liquid is gone, about 5 minutes. Stir in whipping cream (optional) and continue simmering until slightly thickened, 5 to 6 minutes. Season to taste with salt and pepper.

To serve, place a tart shell in the centre of each warmed plate. Spoon mushroom mixture into and around tart shells.

CORNMEAL PASTRY

¾ cup	flour	175 mL
¼ cup	cornmeal	60 mL
½ tsp.	salt	2.5 mL
¼ cup	butter	60 mL
2 Tbsp.	cold water	30 mL

FILLING

¼ cup	butter	60 mL
2	shallots, sliced	2
1 tsp.	minced garlic	5 mL
1 lb.	chanterelle mushrooms	500 g
½ cup	dry sherry	125 mL
½ cup	chicken stock	125 mL
1 tsp.	green Madagascar peppercorns, drained or	5 mL
½ tsp.	pink peppercorns	2.5 mL
1 tsp.	chopped fresh thyme leaves	5 mL
½ cup	whipping cream (optional)	125 mL
	Salt and freshly ground black pepper	

4 individual tarts

Oyster Stew with Leeks and White Vermouth

2 Tbsp.	butter	30 mL
1	medium leek, white part only, thinly sliced	1
12	large fresh shucked beach oysters and juices	12
½ cup	white vermouth	125 mL
1 Tbsp.	lemon zest	15 mL
½ cup	whipping cream	125 mL
	Salt and freshly ground black pepper	
¼ cup	chopped fresh chives	60 mL

4 servings

You can vary the sauce by allowing the cream to reduce to the thickness that you prefer. This offers a great deal of flexibility in how the dish is served. A thinner sauce makes this dish an excellent rich soup, a meal in itself. A slightly thicker sauce makes the stew a delicious starter or even a lunch dish if you serve it ladled over a piece of toast and sprinkled with a small amount of freshly grated Parmesan cheese.

TO MAKE Melt butter in a frying pan on medium heat. Sauté leek until softened, 2 to 3 minutes. Add oysters and their juices; cook until they just begin to plump up, about 1 minute.

Deglaze the pan by adding vermouth and stirring to loosen the browned bits on the bottom. Add lemon zest and whipping cream. Bring to a boil on medium heat, then turn down to medium-low; simmer, uncovered, until oysters are slightly firm to the touch, about 5 minutes. Season with salt and pepper.

To serve, ladle 3 oysters and some sauce into each warmed soup bowl and top with some of the cooked leek. Sprinkle with chopped chives.

Oyster stew with leeks and white vermouth >

Tea-smoked Duck Breast with
Shiitake Mushrooms and Green Tea Vinaigrette

VINAIGRETTE

½ cup	rice vinegar	125 mL
2 Tbsp.	green tea leaves	30 mL
1 tsp.	grated fresh ginger	5 mL
1 Tbsp.	honey	15 mL
1 cup	sunflower oil	250 mL
	Salt and freshly ground black pepper	

SMOKED DUCK

2 Tbsp.	Szechuan peppercorns	30 mL
2 Tbsp.	fennel seeds	30 mL
2 Tbsp.	coriander seeds	30 mL
1 Tbsp.	ground cardamom	15 mL
1 Tbsp.	ground star anise	15 mL
1 tsp.	ground cinnamon	5 mL
½ cup	salt	125 mL
1 cup	brown sugar	250 mL
2	duck breast halves	2
½ cup	white sugar	125 mL
½ cup	black tea leaves	125 mL
½ cup	rice	125 mL
12	shiitake mushrooms, stems removed	12
1 Tbsp.	sesame oil	15 mL
2 cups	spinach leaves	500 mL

4 servings

This recipe has many steps, but it is not difficult—and the result is definitely worth the time. The smoked duck breasts freeze very well and are handy to have ready for a last-minute appetizer.

Using tea to smoke food is a method that has been used for centuries in China, and it is actually the easiest way to hot smoke food at home; it both cooks and smokes at the same time. We use an old saucepan and an 8-inch/20-cm bamboo steamer that fits snugly over it. Line the saucepan with a double layer of aluminum foil, so that the smoking mixture doesn't stick to the pan and can be removed easily once it cools. After you take the smoked duck out of the steamer, set the saucepan outside to cool off and to let the smoke escape.

TO MAKE VINAIGRETTE Combine rice vinegar, green tea leaves and ginger in a bowl. Cover and let sit overnight.

Place vinegar mixture and honey in a blender or food processor, and run while slowly adding sunflower oil. Season to taste with salt and pepper. Strain and set aside.

TO SMOKE DUCK Grind together peppercorns, fennel, coriander, cardamom, star anise and cinnamon in a spice mill or coffee grinder. Transfer spice mixture to a bowl; stir in salt and brown sugar. Coat duck breasts with spice mixture and place them in a covered dish. Cure in the refrigerator for 24 hours.

Line a saucepan with a double layer of aluminum foil. Add white sugar, then top with black tea leaves and rice. Place a snug-fitting bamboo steamer over the saucepan.

Wipe excess curing mixture from duck breasts and place them inside the steamer. Place the saucepan on medium-low heat and smoke duck breasts for 15 minutes on each side. Chill in the refrigerator before serving.

TO ASSEMBLE Cut an "x" in the top of each shiitake mushroom and sauté in sesame oil in a frying pan on medium-high heat until tender, 2 to 3 minutes.

Bring a pot of salted water to a boil. Add spinach leaves and blanch for about 30 seconds. Rinse well in a colander under cold running water and drain.

Cut duck breasts at a 45-degree angle into slices ⅛ inch/3 mm thick.

To serve, arrange slices of duck in a circle on each plate. Top each serving with one shiitake mushroom, an eighth of the spinach, another shiitake mushroom, an eighth of the spinach and then another shiitake mushroom. Drizzle with vinaigrette.

Roasted Pear and Goat Cheese Phyllo Pastries

These stuffed pastries make elegant appetizers. They can also be made in greater quantities to be served as part of a warm hors d'oeuvre platter.

TO MAKE Preheat the oven to 400°F/200°C and line two baking sheets with parchment paper.

Peel and core pears, then cut them in half. Place pear halves, cut side down, on one of the prepared baking sheets. Brush with half of the melted butter, then season with salt and pepper.

Roast until golden brown and tender, about 30 minutes. Remove from the oven and allow to cool. Leave the oven on.

Fold each sheet of phyllo pastry lengthwise twice (so that they are a quarter of their original width). Brush with the remaining melted butter.

Cut pear halves in half, then slice thinly from the stem end, leaving the bottoms attached.

Place a pear piece on each phyllo sheet and top with 1 Tbsp./15 mL goat cheese. Fold pastry over pear and cheese to form triangles. Place on the second prepared baking sheet and bake until pastry is golden and slightly puffed, about 12 minutes.

To serve as an appetizer, place pastry triangles in pairs on warmed plates.

To serve as an hors d'oeuvre, arrange pastry triangles on a warmed platter.

2	Bartlett or Anjou pears	2
2 Tbsp.	butter, melted	30 mL
	Salt and freshly ground black pepper	
4 oz.	fresh goat cheese	125 g
8	sheets frozen phyllo pastry, thawed	8

4 servings

< Tea-smoked duck breast with shiitake mushrooms and green tea vinaigrette (recipe page 24)

Chicken Liver and Green Peppercorn Pâté
with Herb Toast

1 lb.	chicken or duck livers	500 g
1 cup	non-vintage port	250 mL
¼ cup	butter	60 mL
½ cup	shallots, sliced	125 mL
2	garlic cloves, minced	2
¼ cup	green Madagascar peppercorns, drained	60 mL
½ cup	whipping cream	125 mL
2 oz.	brandy	60 mL
1 Tbsp.	chopped fresh thyme	15 mL
2 Tbsp.	chopped fresh parsley	30 mL
	Salt and freshly ground black pepper	

This spicy pâté can also be served as a part of an hors d'oeuvre platter selection. The pâté can be made a day or two ahead; this will also allow the flavours to blend together. I like to use an inexpensive non-vintage port for this recipe.

Madagascar green peppercorns, which come packed in brine, are available in specialty markets and food shops.

TO MAKE PÂTÉ Place livers and port in a bowl. Cover and marinate overnight in the refrigerator.

Drain livers, reserving port.

Melt butter in a frying pan on medium-high heat. Sauté livers (partially cover pan to prevent hot splatters) until browned, 5 to 6 minutes. Add shallots and garlic and sauté until tender, about 3 minutes. Add reserved port and simmer, uncovered, on medium-high heat, until liquid is reduced by 80 per cent, about 10 minutes. Remove from the heat and allow to cool for 15 minutes.

Transfer liver mixture to a blender or food processor, then add green peppercorns. Purée until smooth, slowly adding whipping cream, brandy, thyme and parsley. Season to taste with salt and pepper.

Line a 2-cup/500-mL loaf pan or terrine mold with plastic wrap. Place liver mixture in pan, then cover and chill overnight in the refrigerator before serving. (Pâté can be made ahead and will keep in the refrigerator for 4 to 5 days.)

HERB TOAST Preheat the oven to 350°F/175°C and line a baking sheet with parchment paper.

Cut baguette at a slight angle into 16 to 24 slices (4 slices per serving), ¼ inch/6 mm thick. Combine olive oil, parsley, thyme and garlic in a bowl. Brush herb mixture onto baguette slices. Arrange on the prepared baking sheet and bake until golden brown, about 15 minutes.

To serve as an appetizer, use a hot sharp knife to cut pâté into slices ½ inch/1 cm thick. Place a slice on each plate, along with 4 slices of herb toast. Garnish with pickled onions or cornichons (optional).

To serve as an hors d'oeuvre, place the pâté whole onto a platter, with slices of herb toast on the side. Garnish with pickled onions or cornichons (optional).

TOAST

1	baguette	1
¼ cup	olive oil	60 mL
1 Tbsp.	chopped fresh parsley	15 mL
1 tsp.	chopped fresh thyme	5 mL
1	garlic clove, minced	1
	Pickled onions or cornichons (gherkins) for garnish, optional	

4 to 6 servings

Oysters on the Half Shell with Apple Cider–Shallot Vinaigrette and Other Garnishes

Traditionally, oysters are best in the winter or months with an "r" in them, but now we can enjoy fresh oysters year-round, thanks to modern refrigeration and deep-water cultivation.

To shuck oysters, you need a special oyster knife. There are two ways to open an oyster. You can insert the point of the knife either into the ribbon-like side or into the hinge, then lever the shell open. The method that I prefer to use is the latter. To protect yourself, take a thick towel, fold it double, and hold the oyster tightly in the fold while you shuck it.

Shucked oysters are best served on the half shell on a bed of crushed ice. The accompaniments depend on personal preferences. For that special romantic meal, I pull out the stops and serve all of them.

TO MAKE MIGNONETTE Peel and finely chop shallot. Combine shallot with apple cider vinegar in a bowl. Cover and refrigerate for 1 hour to allow the flavours to develop.

SEAFOOD COCKTAIL SAUCE Mix together tomato ketchup, horseradish and Worcestershire sauce in a bowl.

To serve, place shucked oysters on half shells. Arrange 6 of the shells on a bed of crushed ice on each chilled plate. Place small bowls of lemon wedges, grated horseradish, mignonette and seafood cocktail sauce beside it.

24	fresh small deep-shelled oysters	24
	Lemon wedges, cut at the last minute	
	Fresh horseradish root, grated	

MIGNONETTE

1	shallot	1
½ cup	apple cider vinegar	125 mL

SEAFOOD COCKTAIL SAUCE

½ cup	tomato ketchup	125 mL
1 tsp.	grated fresh horseradish root	5 mL
1 tsp.	Worcestershire sauce	5 mL

4 servings

< Oysters on the half shell with apple cider–shallot vinaigrette and other garnishes

Scallops in Rice Paper with Sesame-Ginger Dressing

SCALLOPS

1	large carrot, grated	1
4	green onions, finely chopped	4
8	sheets rice paper	8
16	large scallops (1 lb./500 g)	16
	Salt and freshly ground black pepper	
1	bunch Swiss chard, destemmed	1

DRESSING

1 tsp.	grated fresh ginger	5 mL
2 Tbsp.	sesame oil	30 mL
2 Tbsp.	rice vinegar	30 mL
1 Tbsp.	soy sauce	15 mL

4 servings

This recipe for scallops with an Asian influence was inspired by a family trip to Beijing a few years ago. We loved all the different foods and the flavours that we were introduced to in China, and ever since then we have frequent cravings for Asian food.

Rice paper is sold in round sheets 8 inches/20 cm in diameter. To soften them for use, soak the sheets in warm water for a minute. Soak the sheets just one at a time as you use them; otherwise, they can become too soft and tear. You can find the rice paper, sesame oil and rice vinegar at Asian food stores.

TO MAKE SCALLOPS Combine carrot and green onions in a bowl.

Soak 1 sheet of rice paper in warm water for 1 minute and place on a work surface. Place 2 scallops in the centre of the rice paper. Season with salt and pepper, then top with 1 Tbsp./15 mL of carrot mixture. Make the rice paper into a package: fold up the bottom, fold the sides in, then fold down the top. Place seam-side down on a tray. Repeat the process for the remaining scallops.

Place a large bamboo steamer on top of a saucepan half full of water. Bring water to a boil on medium-high heat. In the meantime, chop chard coarsely. When water is boiling, arrange chard to cover the inside bottom of the steamer. Place scallop packages on top of chard. Cover and steam over simmering water until just cooked, 3 to 5 minutes.

DRESSING Whisk together ginger, sesame oil, rice vinegar and soy sauce in a bowl.

To serve, remove scallop packages from the steamer. Divide chard among warmed plates and place two scallop packages on each. Drizzle dressing over everything.

Potted Shrimp Infused with Savoury Herbs and Garlic

Potting is an old method of preserving food by sealing it in butter or fat, a process similar to preparing duck confit. This recipe takes me back to my childhood, when occasionally we would have potted shrimp on toasted fingers of bread as part of an afternoon tea party. We also used to have sardines served in a similar way with lemon.

TO MAKE Melt butter in a frying pan on medium heat. Sauté garlic until lightly coloured, about 2 minutes. Stir in thyme, parsley, salt and mustard; remove from the stove.

Spoon shrimp into ramekins and pour butter mixture over top. Cover and chill thoroughly in the refrigerator before serving. (Will keep refrigerated for 4 to 5 days.)

To serve, place ramekins on plates, with toast fingers (or sliced baguette) on the side.

¼ cup	butter	60 mL
1 tsp.	chopped garlic	5 mL
1 tsp.	chopped fresh thyme leaves	5 mL
1 tsp.	chopped fresh parsley	5 mL
	Pinch of salt	
	Pinch of grainy mustard	
8 oz.	fresh hand-peeled shrimp	250 g
	Toast fingers or sliced baguette	

4 ramekins, each 4 oz./125 mL

Spicy Spinach, Watercress and
Asian Pear Soup with Poached Oysters

6	oysters in the shell	6
¼ cup	butter or olive oil	60 mL
1	chopped leek, white part only	1
1 cup	chopped celery	250 mL
1	Asian pear, peeled, cored and chopped	1
1	bunch spinach, stems removed	1
1	bunch watercress, stems removed	1
3 cups	chicken stock	750 mL
1 cup	whipping cream	250 mL
	Sea salt	
	Hot sauce	
	Extra-virgin olive oil	

4 to 6 servings

At least twice a week, I have a bowl of soup for lunch, and I usually slide a fresh oyster or two into it, regardless of the flavour. Then I give it a quick simmer, and that's it. This combination of sweet pear, spicy peppery greens and oysters is one of my favourites.

TO MAKE Shuck oysters (see page 31), being careful to save their juices. Cut oysters into quarters.

Melt butter (or heat olive oil) in a soup pot on medium-high heat. Add leek, celery and pear. Cover and cook until transparent and tender, about 5 minutes. Stir in spinach and watercress. Add chicken stock. Bring to a boil, then turn down the heat to medium; simmer, uncovered, for about 20 minutes. Remove from the stove and allow to cool for 15 minutes.

Purée in a blender or food processor until smooth. Pour into a large saucepan, stir in whipping cream and gently reheat. Add oysters and their juices and cook on medium heat until done, about 5 minutes. Season to taste with sea salt and a few drops of hot sauce.

To serve, ladle soup into warmed bowls and drizzle with a small slick of extra-virgin olive oil.

Cream of Asparagus Soup with Goat Cheese Toast

I love fresh asparagus any way that it's prepared. Thick white European asparagus is delicious, but it is expensive and hard to find. Green asparagus is readily available at local markets in the springtime. This soup can be made using either of these varieties.

TO MAKE SOUP Trim off and discard about 2 inches/5 cm from the tough base of asparagus. Peel stalks, then chop coarsely.

Melt butter in a soup pot on medium heat. Sauté asparagus, onion, celery and potato until soft, about 5 minutes. Add stock and bring to a boil, then turn down the heat to low; simmer, uncovered, for 30 to 40 minutes. Remove from the stove and allow to cool for 15 minutes.

Purée in a blender or food processor. Pour into a large saucepan and stir in whipping cream. Season to taste with salt and pepper.

TOAST Preheat the broiler on high heat.

Slice 4 rounds off the baguette, ¼ inch/6 mm thick. Place the slices on a baking sheet. (Use the remainder of the bread for sandwiches or to make croutons.)

Cut goat cheese into 4 slices and place one on top of each slice of bread. Broil until cheese is golden brown, 3 to 4 minutes.

To serve, reheat soup and ladle into warmed bowls. Top each with a goat cheese toast.

SOUP

1 lb.	asparagus	500 g
2 Tbsp.	butter	30 mL
1	medium sweet onion (Walla Walla), chopped	1
2	celery ribs, chopped	2
1	medium potato, peeled, 1-inch/ 2.5-cm dice	1
4 cups	chicken or vegetable stock	1 L
1 cup	whipping cream	250 mL
	Salt and freshly ground black pepper	

TOAST

1	baguette	1
3 oz.	goat cheese	90 g

4 servings

Confetti Vegetable Soup

2 Tbsp.	olive oil	30 mL
2	garlic cloves, chopped	2
1 tsp.	grated fresh ginger	5 mL
½ cup	carrot, ¹⁄₁₆-inch/2-mm dice	125 mL
1 cup	sweet onion, peeled, ¹⁄₁₆-inch/2-mm dice	250 mL
½ cup	celery, ¹⁄₁₆-inch/2-mm dice	125 mL
½ cup	potato, peeled, ¹⁄₁₆-inch/2-mm dice	125 mL
1 cup	squash, peeled, ¹⁄₁₆-inch/2-mm dice	250 mL
4 cups	chicken or vegetable stock	1 L
1 tsp.	lemon zest	5 mL
1	bay leaf	1
1 Tbsp.	chopped fresh dill	15 mL
1 Tbsp.	chopped fresh parsley	15 mL
	Salt and freshly ground black pepper	

4 to 6 servings

This soup was inspired by a recent trip to India. When I had lunch at a restaurant in the city of Dehradun, the waiter insisted that I order the vegetable soup. What arrived was a wonderfully simple bowl of broth filled to the brim with vegetables cut into the smallest pieces you could ever imagine; the culinary term for this is "brunoise." Here is my version of that soup. Although cutting up the vegetables this small is a lot of work even for a professional chef, it's also a good form of therapy. So go ahead and cut, cut cut.

TO MAKE Heat olive oil in a soup pot on medium heat. Add garlic, ginger, carrot, onion, celery, potato and squash. Cover and cook until tender, 5 to 6 minutes.

Add stock, lemon zest and bay leaf. Bring to a boil on high heat. Turn down the heat to medium and simmer, uncovered, for 20 to 30 minutes. Skim off any foam that comes to the surface. Add dill and parsley. Remove and discard the bay leaf. Season to taste with salt and pepper.

To serve, ladle soup into warmed bowls. This soup looks so beautiful by itself that it doesn't need any garnish.

Confetti vegetable soup >

Roasted Tomato Summer Soup

8	large ripe heirloom tomatoes, quartered	8
2	medium sweet onions, coarsely chopped	2
2	celery ribs, peeled and coarsely chopped	2
6	garlic cloves	6
1	whole chili pepper (green or red)	1
1 tsp.	fennel seeds	5 mL
½ tsp.	turmeric	2.5 mL
½ tsp.	ground cumin	2.5 mL
4 Tbsp.	olive oil	60 mL
1 Tbsp.	honey, melted (optional)	15 mL
4 cups	vegetable or chicken stock	1 L
	Salt and freshly ground black pepper	
	Fresh chopped basil or cilantro for garnish	

4 to 6 servings

Try to find the biggest, ripest tomatoes you can for this soup—just about any variety or colour will do. I prefer the heirloom tomatoes sold at farmers' markets throughout the summer months because they are so juicy and taste so much better than many of the varieties sold in stores. Roasting the tomatoes first makes them even sweeter.

This soup is very versatile. You can serve it either hot or cold. You can even serve it as a sauce alongside steamed summer vegetables or barbecued seafood.

TO MAKE Preheat the oven to 350°F/175°C.

Place tomatoes, onions, celery, garlic and chili pepper into a roasting pan. Combine fennel seeds, turmeric, cumin, olive oil and honey (optional) in a bowl. Add to tomato mixture and toss gently to coat evenly with oil. Roast in the oven until vegetables are tender and caramelized, about 45 minutes.

Transfer vegetables to a soup pot. Pour in stock, then season to taste with salt and pepper. Bring to a boil on high heat, then turn down the heat to medium-low. Cover and simmer for about 40 minutes. Remove from the stove and allow to cool for 15 minutes.

Purée in a blender or food processor. Pour into a large saucepan and reheat gently.

To serve, ladle soup into warmed bowls and garnish with chopped basil or cilantro.

Chilled Peach and Honey Soup

This golden fruit soup really is a celebration of the summer season. Perfect summer weather in the Okanagan Valley of British Columbia produces magnificent tree-ripened peaches. We then poach them in a syrup made using herbs, spices and a fruity local wine, such as a Riesling or Gewürztraminer.

TO MAKE Fill a bowl with ice-cold water. Next, bring a pot of water to a boil. Score peaches with a paring knife and place them in boiling water for 15 to 30 seconds, then plunge them into ice-cold water.

Using a paring knife, remove and discard skin from peaches. Run a knife down through the seam of the peach until you hit the stone. Turn the knife to remove the stone.

In a soup pot, combine peach halves, white wine, honey, ginger, cinnamon stick and lemon verbena. Bring to a boil on medium-high heat, then turn down the heat to low; cover and simmer for 30 minutes. Pick out and discard lemon verbena leaves and cinnamon stick. Remove from the stove and allow to cool for 15 minutes.

Purée in a blender or food processor until smooth. Transfer to a covered container and chill in the refrigerator.

To serve, add sparkling mineral water to peach purée and whisk together. Ladle soup into chilled bowls and garnish with a dollop of plain yogurt and a sprinkling of mint.

4	large peaches	4
1 cup	fruity white wine	250 mL
½ cup	liquid honey	125 mL
1 tsp.	grated fresh ginger	5 mL
1	stick cinnamon	1
3 or 4	leaves fresh lemon verbena	3 or 4
2 cups	sparkling mineral water	500 mL
	Plain yogurt for garnish	
	Chopped fresh mint leaves for garnish	

4 servings

Chilled Blueberry Soup with Tarragon and Mascarpone

2 cups	fresh blueberries	500 mL
2	lemons, zest and juice	2
½ cup	white sugar or honey	125 mL
1 cup	dry white wine	250 mL
1 cup	water	250 mL
1 Tbsp.	fresh tarragon leaves	15 mL
1 tsp.	fresh thyme leaves	5 mL
1 cup	mascarpone cheese	250 mL
	Plain yogurt for garnish	

4 servings

Fresh blueberries are just so great this time of year.

This unusual but delicious summer soup was the inspiration of Dawne Gourley, formerly a pastry chef and soup maker at Bishop's. I particularly like the flavour combination of fresh tarragon and lemon. Also, the colour is sensational. You can also make this soup using other fruits such as plums or cherries (remember to pit them first).

TO MAKE Place blueberries, lemon zest and juice, sugar (or honey), white wine, water, tarragon and thyme into a soup pot. Bring to a boil on medium-high heat; simmer, uncovered, until fruit is soft, about 5 minutes. Remove from the stove and allow to cool for 15 minutes.

Transfer to a blender or food processor and add mascarpone cheese. Purée until smooth. Refrigerate until completely chilled.

To serve, ladle soup into slightly chilled bowls and garnish with a swirl of yogurt in the centre.

Sweet Corn and Celery Root Chowder

This all-vegetable soup makes a hearty beginning to a festive fall meal. Making the corn broth is a bit of work, but you can prepare it ahead of time; save the corn kernels from making the broth for this soup. When you taste the sweet flavours of the corn broth and the soft subtle texture of the celery root, which go so well together, you'll agree that it's worth the effort. I like to serve it with hot crusty bread.

TO MAKE Melt butter in a soup pot on medium heat. Sauté onion, celery root, red peppers, garlic and thyme until onion is translucent, about 5 minutes.

Deglaze the pot by adding sherry and stirring to loosen the browned bits on the bottom. Add corn broth and bring to a boil on high heat, then turn down the heat to low; simmer, uncovered, until vegetables are cooked thoroughly, about 30 minutes. Remove from the stove and allow to cool for 15 minutes.

Purée in a blender or food processor and return to the pot. Stir in corn kernels and whipping cream. Bring to a boil, then turn down the heat to low; simmer, uncovered, for 10 minutes. Season to taste with salt and pepper.

To serve, ladle soup into warmed bowls.

2 Tbsp.	butter	30 mL
½ cup	onion, ¼-inch/ 6-mm dice	125 mL
1 cup	celery root, peeled, ¼-inch/6-mm dice	250 mL
1 cup	red peppers, ¼-inch/ 6-mm dice	250 mL
2	garlic cloves, chopped	2
2 Tbsp.	chopped fresh thyme	30 mL
½ cup	dry sherry	125 mL
4 cups	sweet corn broth (page 165)	1 L
2 cups	corn kernels	500 mL
½ cup	whipping cream	125 mL
	Salt and freshly ground black pepper	

4 to 6 servings

Golden Beet Soup with Orange and Dill Sour Cream

GARNISH

4 Tbsp.	sour cream	60 mL
1 tsp.	orange zest	5 mL
1 tsp.	chopped fresh dill	5 mL

SOUP

1 lb.	beets	500 g
2 Tbsp.	olive oil	30 mL
1	medium onion, ¼-inch/6-mm dice	1
1	celery rib, ¼-inch/ 6-mm dice	1
1 cup	freshly squeezed orange juice	250 mL
3 cups	vegetable stock	750 mL
	Salt and freshly ground black pepper	

4 servings

This is my version of the classic Russian/Polish soup called borscht. For this recipe, I use golden beets, which have an amazing colour. They taste about the same as their purple cousins, but they don't stain. After cooking beets, the skin slips off easily. If you can't find golden beets, just use one of the many other different varieties of beets to prepare this soup.

TO MAKE GARNISH Mix together sour cream, orange zest and dill in a bowl. Cover and refrigerate until ready to serve.

SOUP Put beets into a soup pot and cover with cold water. Put a lid on the pot and bring to a boil on medium heat; cook until tender, about 40 minutes. Drain and allow to cool. When beets have cooled, remove and discard their skins. Grate coarsely.

Heat olive oil in a soup pot on medium-high heat. Sauté onion and celery until tender, about 5 minutes. Add cooked grated beets, orange juice and stock. Bring to a boil and stir well. Season to taste with salt and pepper. Turn down the heat to low and simmer, uncovered, for about 30 minutes.

To serve, ladle soup into warmed bowls and top each with 1 Tbsp./15 mL of garnish.

Butternut Squash and Apple Soup

It is a sure sign of fall when this soup appears on the restaurant's menu. There are many different varieties of squashes and apples to choose from, but I love to use butternut squash, as its bright orange flesh tastes smooth and creamy when cooked like this. Both the squash and apple have their own kinds of sweetness, but the apple provides a lovely fresh acidity to balance the richness of the soup. My favourite apple varieties for this soup are Fuji, Gala and Macintosh. I like to garnish the soup with thin slices of grilled apple.

TO MAKE Heat olive oil and butter in a soup pot on medium heat. Sauté onion and garlic until translucent, about 5 minutes. Add cumin, squash and apple. Cook, stirring gently to coat apple and squash evenly with oil, 2 to 3 minutes.

Deglaze the pan by adding sherry and stirring to loosen the browned bits on the bottom. Add stock. Bring to a boil on medium-high heat, then turn down the heat to low; simmer, uncovered, until vegetables are tender, about 45 minutes. Stir in coconut milk. Remove from the stove and allow to cool for 15 minutes.

Purée in a blender or food processor until smooth. Season to taste with salt. Pour into a soup pot and reheat gently.

To serve, ladle soup into warmed bowls.

2 Tbsp.	olive oil	30 mL
2 Tbsp.	butter	30 mL
1	medium onion, ½-inch/1-cm dice	1
2	garlic cloves, minced	2
1 Tbsp.	ground cumin	15 mL
1 lb.	squash, peeled, 1-inch/2.5-cm dice	500 g
2	apples, cored, peeled, ½-inch/ 1-cm thick slices	2
¼ cup	dry sherry	60 mL
4 cups	chicken or vegetable stock	1 L
1	can coconut milk (14 oz./398 mL)	1
	Salt	

4 to 6 servings

Wild Mushroom Soup with Thyme Chantilly

THYME CHANTILLY

½ cup	whipping cream	125 mL
1 tsp.	chopped fresh thyme	5 mL
	Salt and freshly ground black pepper	

SOUP

2 Tbsp.	butter	30 mL
1	large onion, sliced	1
2	garlic cloves, sliced	2
2	celery ribs, sliced	2
1 lb.	wild mushrooms, sliced	500 g
½ cup	dry sherry	125 mL
4 cups	chicken stock	1 L
2	sprigs fresh rosemary	2
½ cup	whipping cream	125 mL
	Salt and freshly ground black pepper	

4 to 6 servings

Wild mushrooms always remind me of my childhood growing up in Wales. Early in the morning when the grass was still damp with dew, we would head off to pick mushrooms, then come home and fry them in butter for breakfast or use them to make soup. Autumn is the time when we seem to get the most variety of wild mushrooms, and chanterelles are the type that I like to use. They have a wonderful woodsy smell to them, and are also the most common variety sold in specialty markets at this time of year.

TO MAKE THYME CHANTILLY Whip cream to stiff peaks in a bowl and fold in thyme. Season to taste with salt and pepper. Cover and refrigerate until ready to serve.

SOUP Melt butter in a soup pot on medium heat. Sauté onion, garlic and celery until tender, about 5 minutes. Add mushrooms and sauté until they are soft, about 5 minutes.

Deglaze the pan by adding sherry and stirring to loosen the browned bits on the bottom. Add stock and rosemary. Bring to a boil on medium-high heat, then turn down the heat to low; simmer, uncovered, for 45 minutes. Stir in whipping cream and simmer for 10 more minutes. Pick out and discard rosemary. Remove from the stove and allow to cool for 15 minutes.

Purée in a blender or food processor and strain. Season to taste with salt and pepper. Pour into a large saucepan and reheat gently.

To serve, ladle soup into warmed bowls and top each with a dollop of Thyme Chantilly.

Russet Potato, Leek and Roast Garlic Soup

This lovely, basic soup is practically a national dish to most Celts. Try to make it using organic potatoes and leeks because they taste so much better. Instead of the russets, you can use almost any kind of large potatoes. The only guilty ingredient in this recipe is the whipping cream. Instead of blending the cream into the soup, you can whip it separately and use it as a topping. I like to serve home-made sea-salted potato chips with this soup.

TO MAKE Heat vegetable oil in a soup pot on medium heat. Sauté onion and garlic until golden, 2 to 3 minutes. Add leek and cook until softened, about 5 minutes.

Deglaze the pan by adding sherry and stirring to loosen the browned bits on the bottom. Add stock (or water) and potatoes. Bring to a boil on high heat, then turn down the heat to medium; simmer, uncovered, until potatoes are soft, about 45 minutes. Stir in whipping cream (or whip and use as garnish). Season to taste with salt and pepper. Remove from the stove and allow to cool for 15 minutes.

Purée in a blender or food processor. Pour into a large saucepan and reheat gently.

To serve, ladle into warmed bowls and drizzle with a few drops of truffle oil (optional).

¼ cup	vegetable oil	60 mL
1	medium onion, sliced	1
12	garlic cloves	12
1	medium leek, white part only, sliced	1
½ cup	dry sherry	125 mL
6 cups	vegetable stock or water	1.5 L
2 lb.	russet potatoes, peeled, 1-inch/2.5-cm dice	1 kg
½ cup	whipping cream	125 mL
	Salt and freshly ground black pepper	
	Truffle oil for garnish, optional	

4 to 6 servings

Dungeness Crab Chowder with Lemon Grass and Coconut

This decadent soup is a perfect start to a special-occasion meal. Fresh Dungeness crabmeat combined with these Asian ingredients makes for a real taste treat. A less expensive but delicious seafood alternative is to use 2-inch/5-cm cubes of fresh red snapper fillets, but make sure that you remove all the bones first.

TO MAKE Melt butter in a soup pot on medium heat. Sauté garlic, ginger, lemon grass, onion, celery, fennel, and red and yellow peppers until tender, about 5 minutes.

Deglaze the pot by adding sherry and stirring to loosen the browned bits on the bottom. Add stock, coconut milk, chili pepper, bay leaf, lime juice and basil. Bring to a boil on high heat, then turn down the heat to medium; simmer, uncovered, for 30 minutes. Add crabmeat and continue simmering for a further 10 minutes. Remove and discard chili pepper and bay leaf. Season with salt and pepper.

To serve, ladle soup into in warmed bowls.

2 Tbsp.	butter	30 mL
2	garlic cloves, minced	2
1 Tbsp.	finely chopped fresh ginger	15 mL
2 tsp.	finely chopped lemon grass	10 mL
½ cup	onion, ¼-inch/ 6-mm dice	125 mL
½ cup	celery, ¼-inch/ 6-mm dice	125 mL
½ cup	fennel bulb, peeled, ¼-inch/6-mm dice	125 mL
½ cup	red pepper, ¼-inch/ 6-mm dice	125 mL
½ cup	yellow pepper, ¼-inch/6-mm dice	125 mL
½ cup	dry sherry	125 mL
2 cups	fish stock	500 mL
1	can coconut milk (14 oz./398 mL)	1
1	whole chili pepper	1
1	bay leaf	1
2 Tbsp.	lime juice	30 mL
3	fresh basil leaves, chopped	3
½ lb.	cooked Dungeness crabmeat	250 g
1½ tsp.	salt	7.5 mL
½ tsp.	freshly ground black pepper	2.5 mL

4 servings

< *Top:* Curried broccoli soup with cucumber-mint raita (recipe page 50)

Bottom: Dungeness crab chowder with lemon grass and coconut

Curried Broccoli Soup with Cucumber-Mint Raita

½ cup	grated English cucumber	125 mL
1½ tsp.	chopped fresh mint leaves	7.5 mL
½ cup	plain yogurt	125 mL
½ tsp.	ground cumin	2.5 mL
	Pinch of salt	

I have learned quite a bit about curry from my friend and restaurateur Vikram Vij. He tells me that, in India, every family grinds and blends its own mixture, which is called *garam masala* or "hot spices"; it's also sold in Asian food stores. This is usually added at the last minute, as hot spices can turn bitter if cooked too much.

Set your table with a beautiful hand-printed Indian tablecloth and a brass candleholder, put on a Ravi Shankar CD and escape to another world over this bowl of what I like to think of as a green sea of soup. The Cucumber-Mint Raita adds an oasis of coolness. You can also make this soup using fresh zucchini.

TO MAKE RAITA Combine cucumber, mint, yogurt, cumin and salt in a bowl. Cover and refrigerate for 1 hour before serving to allow the flavours to develop.

SOUP Melt butter (or heat vegetable oil) in a soup pot on medium-high heat. Add onion, celery, garlic and ginger. Cover and cook until vegetables are transparent and partially cooked, about 5 minutes. Stir in turmeric, coriander, chili pepper, broccoli and lentils. Add stock and coconut milk. Bring to a boil, then turn down the heat to medium; simmer, uncovered, for 45 minutes. Remove from the stove and season with garam masala, salt and pepper. Allow to cool for 15 minutes.

Purée in a blender or food processor until smooth. Pour into a large saucepan and reheat gently.

To serve, ladle soup into warmed bowls and top with a spoonful or two of raita.

SOUP

2 Tbsp.	butter or vegetable oil	30 mL
1 cup	onion, 1-inch/ 2.5-cm dice	250 mL
1 cup	celery, 1-inch/ 2.5-cm dice	250 mL
2	garlic cloves, chopped	2
1 Tbsp.	grated fresh ginger	15 mL
1 tsp.	ground turmeric	5 mL
1 tsp.	ground coriander	5 mL
1	small green chili pepper, seeded and chopped	1
1	head of fresh broccoli, chopped	1
¼ cup	green lentils, soaked in cold water for 2 hours	60 mL
2 cups	vegetable or chicken stock	500 mL
1	can coconut milk (14 oz./398 mL)	1
1 tsp.	garam masala	5 mL
	Salt and freshly ground black pepper	

4 servings

AUTUMN

Steamed Artichokes Stuffed with
Chicken, Apple and Celery Salad 65

Autumn Greens with
Raspberry Vinaigrette and
Toasted Pumpkin Seeds 67

SPRING

Avocado and Orange Salad with
Balsamic Vinaigrette and
Parmesan Curls 54

Spinach Salad with
Creamy Dijon Dressing 56

Warm Shiitake Mushroom and
Watercress Salad with Pancetta 57

Butter Lettuce Quarters with
Creamy Citrus Dressing and
Warm Garlic Toast 59

WINTER

Cabbage-Carrot Slaw with
Blue Cheese and Walnuts 68

Beet Salad with Raspberry Vinaigrette
and Goat Cheese 69

SUMMER

Potato Salad with Roasted Red Peppers,
Capers and Dill 60

Summer Greens with Basil Buttermilk
Dressing and Fresh Raspberries 61

Ahi Tuna Salad with
String Beans and Olives 62

Heirloom Tomato and Sweet Onion Salad
with Balsamic Syrup and Basil Oil 64

Avocado and Orange Salad with Balsamic Vinaigrette and Parmesan Curls

2	avocados	2
2	oranges	2
1 cup	thinly shaved fennel bulb	250 mL
1 Tbsp.	balsamic vinegar	15 mL
3 Tbsp.	extra-virgin olive oil	45 mL
	Salt and freshly ground black pepper	
8 to 12	Parmesan cheese curls	8 to 12

4 servings

The combination of buttery ripe avocado, sweet citrus juices and crunchy, thinly shaved fennel bulb makes this salad a perfect accompaniment to a seafood dish such as Chardonnay-poached Prawns with Lemon and Parsley Aïoli (page 79) or Nova Scotia Lobster with Ginger Citrus Sabayon (page 86).

This is a salad to make in the early spring, when citrus fruits are at the peak of their season. For an amazing colour, use blood oranges if available.

TO MAKE Peel avocados, remove pits and cut into slices ½ inch/1 cm thick. Peel oranges and cut into slices ¼ inch/ 6 mm thick.

Place shaved fennel in a bowl and toss together with balsamic vinegar and extra-virgin olive oil. Season to taste with salt and pepper.

To make the Parmesan cheese curls, use a sharp potato or vegetable peeler to shave thin slices off a block of cheese.

Arrange alternating slices of avocado and orange to form a circle on each salad plate. Place some dressed sliced fennel in the centre of each plate and top each with 2 or 3 Parmesan cheese curls.

Avocado and orange salad with balsamic vinaigrette and parmesan curls >

Spinach Salad with Creamy Dijon Dressing

1 Tbsp.	mild Dijon mustard	15 ml
2 Tbsp.	mayonnaise	30 ml
2 Tbsp.	sour cream	30 mL
1 Tbsp.	white wine vinegar	15 mL
	Salt and freshly ground black pepper	
1	bunch spinach	1

4 servings

This easy-to-make creamy Dijon salad dressing is very tasty. You can also use it as a dip for vegetables or seafood such as cracked crab or steamed shrimp; just stir in the juice of a half a lemon.

For a more robust version of this salad, I like to add some crumbled aged white cheddar or blue cheese, and a clove of crushed garlic.

TO MAKE Make dressing by whisking together Dijon mustard, mayonnaise, sour cream and white wine vinegar in a bowl. Season to taste with salt and pepper. If dressing is too thick, add a little more vinegar to thin it. Cover and refrigerate until ready to use. (Will keep in the refrigerator for 3 to 4 days.)

To serve, place spinach in a salad bowl, add dressing and toss to coat spinach leaves evenly.

Warm Shiitake Mushroom and Watercress Salad with Pancetta

From the first time I tasted a warm salad, I loved the concept of hot and cold together. This combination of richly flavoured shiitake mushrooms, sweet and sour vinaigrette and spicy pancetta makes a savoury warm salad.

TO MAKE Preheat the oven to 400°F/200°C and line a baking sheet with parchment paper.

Place pancetta slices on the prepared baking sheet. Bake until golden brown and crispy, about 15 minutes. Remove from the oven and allow to cool.

Cut off and discard mushroom stems. Slice mushrooms coarsely. Cut off and discard watercress stems, wash well and place in a large bowl.

Heat olive oil in a frying pan on medium-high heat. Sauté mushrooms, shallot and garlic until mushrooms are soft and cooked, about 5 minutes. Add mustard, water, sugar (or honey) and apple cider vinegar. Bring to a boil, then remove the pan from the heat. Pour dressing over watercress and toss gently.

To serve, divide watercress among warmed plates and garnish each with a slice of crispy baked pancetta.

4	slices pancetta	4
2 cups	shiitake mushrooms	500 mL
2	bunches watercress	2
2 Tbsp.	olive oil	30 mL
1 Tbsp.	shallot, ¼-inch/ 6-mm dice	15 mL
1	garlic clove, chopped	1
1 Tbsp.	mild Dijon mustard	15 mL
2 Tbsp.	water	30 mL
1 tsp.	sugar or honey	5 mL
¼ cup	apple cider vinegar	60 mL

4 servings

Butter Lettuce Quarters with Creamy Citrus Dressing and Warm Garlic Toast

I love butter lettuce because it is soft and yet crispy. Butter lettuce quarters are also delicious as a hot vegetable, covered and lightly sautéed in a little butter with a chopped shallot until just tender.

TO PREPARE LETTUCE Cut lettuce into quarters, but keep each quarter attached at the bottom so that its leaves stay together. Wash lettuce well and dry in a salad spinner or pat dry with a clean towel. Place lettuce in the refrigerator to chill and get really crispy, for at least 20 minutes.

DRESSING Whisk together mayonnaise, sour cream (or plain yogurt), white wine vinegar and lemon zest in a bowl. Season to taste with salt and pepper. Cover and refrigerate until ready to serve.

TOAST Cut crusts off bread. Place a frying pan on medium-high heat and add butter, olive oil and garlic. When mixture is hot, fry bread slices on both sides until golden brown, 1 to 2 minutes per side. Transfer bread to paper towels to drain off excess oil.

To serve, place butter lettuce quarters in a bowl and toss gently together with the creamy dressing. Place a warm slice of garlic toast on each plate and then carefully lay a lettuce quarter on top. Garnish with chopped chives (optional) and freshly grated Parmesan cheese (optional).

1	head butter lettuce	1
1 Tbsp.	mayonnaise	15 mL
1 Tbsp.	sour cream or plain yogurt	15 mL
1 Tbsp.	white wine vinegar	15 mL
½ tsp.	lemon zest	2.5 mL
	Salt and freshly ground black pepper	
4	square thin slices of bread, white or brown	4
2 Tbsp.	butter	30 mL
2 Tbsp.	olive oil	30 mL
2	garlic cloves, crushed and chopped	2
	Chopped chives for garnish, optional	
	Grated Parmesan cheese for garnish, optional	

4 servings

< Butter lettuce quarters with creamy citrus dressing and warm garlic toast

Potato Salad with Roasted Red Peppers, Capers and Dill

2	red peppers	2
2 lb.	new potatoes	1 kg
3 Tbsp.	red wine vinegar	45 mL
2 Tbsp.	capers, drained and coarsely chopped	30 mL
2 Tbsp.	chopped fresh dill	30 mL
3 Tbsp.	extra-virgin olive oil	45 mL
	Sea salt and freshly ground black pepper	

4 to 6 servings

In one of the meetings to plan this book, our editor, Saeko, described this simple but different potato salad that a friend of hers (Josie Cook) makes all the time. It sounded so good that we wanted to include it. It's very handy for picnics, as it does not use mayonnaise in the dressing.

TO MAKE Roast red peppers, then peel and remove seeds (page 121). Cut into slices about ⅛ × 1 inch/3 × 25 mm.

Place potatoes in a saucepan and cover with cold water. Put the lid on the pan and bring to a simmer on medium-high heat. Cook potatoes until tender, 25 to 30 minutes.

Drain well. While potatoes are still hot, sprinkle evenly with red wine vinegar.

When potatoes have cooled, toss gently with red peppers, capers, dill and extra-virgin olive oil. Season with sea salt and pepper.

Serve at room temperature or chill until ready to serve and bring back up to room temperature before serving. (Keeps for 48 hours in the refrigerator.)

Summer Greens with Basil-Buttermilk Dressing and Fresh Raspberries

This simple and refreshing summer salad uses a light dressing made with fresh basil and buttermilk. The tangy dressing and juicy red raspberries are a perfect complement to the baby lettuces that are available all summer.

TO MAKE Place egg and mustard in a blender or food processor and purée. Slowly add vegetable oil, then basil, until well combined. Add white wine vinegar, then buttermilk. Mix well. Season with salt and freshly ground pepper.

To serve, cut cucumber into slices ⅛ inch/3 mm thick and arrange in a circle on each chilled salad plate. Fill the centre with salad greens and drizzle with dressing. Garnish with raspberries.

DRESSING

1	egg	1
1 tsp.	Dijon mustard	5 mL
½ cup	vegetable oil	175 mL
¼ cup	chopped fresh basil	60 mL
¼ cup	white wine vinegar	60 mL
¼ cup	buttermilk	60 mL
	Salt and freshly ground black pepper	

SALAD

1	English cucumber	1
4 cups	salad greens	1 L
8 oz.	raspberries	250 g

4 servings

Ahi Tuna Salad with String Beans and Olives

¼ cup	olive oil	60 mL
1	shallot, sliced	1
1	garlic clove, chopped	1
2 Tbsp.	sliced sun-dried tomatoes	30 mL
¼ cup	red wine vinegar	60 mL
¼ cup	vegetable oil	60 mL
	Salt and freshly ground black pepper	

SALAD

8 oz.	Ahi tuna, in one piece	250 g
	Sea salt	
2	hard-boiled eggs, peeled and halved	2
24	green beans, blanched	24
24	niçoise or calamata olives	24
4	new potatoes, boiled and sliced	4
	Tobiko (flying fish roe) for garnish, optional	
	Freshly ground black pepper for garnish	

4 servings

This recipe immediately takes me to sun-drenched places like Nice, Naples or Santarini, where it seems like every sidewalk café menu offers a version of this salad. I like to serve it with fresh hot crusty bread; it becomes a meal in itself with a nice cool glass of local white wine.

TO MAKE VINAIGRETTE Heat 1 Tbsp./15 mL of the olive oil in a frying pan on medium heat. Sauté shallot and garlic until soft, 2 to 3 minutes. Add sun-dried tomatoes and red wine vinegar. Remove from the heat, cover and allow to cool to room temperature.

Purée in a blender or food processor, then slowly add the remaining olive oil and vegetable oil. Season to taste with salt and pepper. Set aside.

SALAD Preheat the grill or barbecue on high heat.

Season tuna with sea salt, then grill until rare, about 2 to 3 minutes on each side. Cool in the refrigerator until ready to serve.

To serve, cut tuna into slices ¼ inch/6 mm thick. On each chilled salad plate, arrange half a hard-boiled egg, 6 blanched green beans, 6 olives and 1 sliced potato. Drizzle with vinaigrette. Top each plate with 3 slices of tuna and garnish with tobiko (optional) and freshly ground black pepper.

Ahi tuna salad with string beans and olives >

Heirloom Tomato and Sweet Onion Salad
with Balsamic Syrup and Basil Oil

1 cup	balsamic vinegar	250 mL
1 Tbsp.	salt	15 mL
1 cup	fresh basil leaves	250 mL
½ cup	olive oil	125 mL
1 lb.	assorted heirloom tomatoes	500 g
1	medium sweet onion	1
	Sea salt and freshly ground black pepper	

4 servings

Summer always brings us one of our favourite times of the year—tomato season! For four to six weeks from August to mid-September, we have a multitude of luscious heirloom tomato varieties to cook with. This salad is a celebration of that sunny time, with some very simple yet effective accompaniments to the best tomatoes of the year.

TO MAKE BALSAMIC SYRUP Place balsamic vinegar in a small saucepan on medium heat and bring to a boil. Simmer, uncovered, until vinegar is reduced to ¼ cup/ 60 mL. Allow to cool to room temperature and place in a squeeze bottle. Refrigerate until needed. (Will keep refrigerated for 2 to 3 weeks.)

BASIL OIL Fill a medium saucepan with water, add salt and bring to a boil on medium heat. Blanch basil leaves by plunging into the boiling water for 1 to 2 minutes, then immediately drain in a colander under running cold water. Wring out basil and place in a blender or food processor, add olive oil and blend until mixture is a brilliant green colour. Transfer to a covered container and refrigerate until needed. (Will keep refrigerated for 4 to 5 days.) Before serving, allow basil oil to soften to room temperature for a few minutes. Shake well before serving.

To serve, slice or quarter tomatoes according to size. Peel and slice onion as thinly as possible. Arrange tomatoes attractively on plates and top with onion slices. Drizzle with balsamic syrup and basil oil. Season to taste with sea salt and pepper.

Steamed Artichokes Stuffed with Chicken, Apple and Celery Salad

This simple but elegant salad, a variation on the classic Waldorf, is a good way to use leftover cooked chicken. It makes a great lunch all by itself in the early autumn.

TO MAKE FILLING Cut cooked chicken into slices ¼ inch/ 6 mm thick. Gently mix together chicken slices, onion, apples, celery, grapes, capers and mayonnaise in a bowl. Season to taste with salt and pepper. Chill thoroughly in the refrigerator.

ARTICHOKES Bring a large pot of water to a boil. Add lemon halves and salt. Trim off and discard top and outer leaves of artichokes and place in boiling water. Place a small plate on top of artichokes to keep them submerged. Simmer on medium-low heat until the artichoke bottoms are tender when pierced with a knife, about 20 minutes. Drain artichokes and cool.

Once cool, open centre leaves of artichokes and remove the choke (the centre of the artichoke), taking care to scrape off and discard any hairy bits. Chill thoroughly in the refrigerator.

To serve, fill artichokes with chicken salad and place on chilled plates.

FILLING

2	cooked skinless boneless chicken breast halves	2
1	small red onion, ¼-inch/6-mm dice	1
2	apples, ¼-inch/ 6-mm dice	2
2	celery ribs, ¼-inch/ 6-mm thick slices	2
½ cup	green or red seedless grapes, halved	125 mL
2 Tbsp.	capers, drained	30 mL
½ cup	mayonnaise	125 mL
	Salt and freshly ground black pepper	

ARTICHOKES

2	lemons, halved	2
1 Tbsp.	salt	15 mL
4	artichokes	4

4 servings

Autumn Greens with Raspberry Vinaigrette and Toasted Pumpkin Seeds

These autumn greens tossed with raspberry vinegar dressing and toasted pumpkin seeds make a wonderful crunchy salad. We make this dressing with either grapeseed oil or a nut oil such as walnut or hazelnut.

TO MAKE Place shallot, mustard and raspberry vinegar in a blender or food processor and process until well mixed. Slowly add grapeseed (or walnut) oil and vegetable oil. Season to taste with salt and pepper. Strain.

To serve, toss greens with desired amount of vinaigrette, then arrange on chilled salad plates. Garnish with toasted pumpkin seeds.

1	shallot, sliced	1
½ tsp.	Dijon mustard	2.5 mL
¼ cup	raspberry vinegar	60 mL
½ cup	grapeseed oil or walnut oil	125 mL
¼ cup	vegetable oil	60 mL
	Salt and freshly ground black pepper	
4 cups	autumn salad greens	1 L
½ cup	toasted shelled pumpkin seeds	125 mL

4 servings

< Autumn greens with raspberry vinaigrette
  and toasted pumpkin seeds

Cabbage-Carrot Slaw with Blue Cheese and Walnuts

2 oz.	blue cheese	60 g
½ cup	mayonnaise	125 mL
2 Tbsp.	apple cider vinegar	30 mL
1 tsp.	sugar	5 mL

SALAD

2 cups	shredded green cabbage	500 mL
1 cup	shredded red cabbage	250 mL
1 cup	coarsely grated carrot	250 mL
¼ cup	finely sliced red pepper	60 mL
¼ cup	finely sliced red onion	60 mL
¼ cup	coarsely chopped fresh walnuts	60 mL
	Salt	
	Chopped walnuts for garnish	
	Blue cheese for garnish	

4 to 6 servings

The only that way I can remember eating cabbage before I moved to North America was either boiled to death in the traditional manner or as a late-night fry-up with mashed potatoes (fondly known as Bubble and Squeak). But slaw, being raw, is different. The creamy blue cheese dressing in combination with the finely cut crunchy cabbage and carrot makes for a really full-flavoured salad, a hearty winter alternative to a green salad.

TO MAKE DRESSING Place blue cheese, mayonnaise, apple cider vinegar and sugar in a blender or food processor and purée.

SALAD Place green cabbage, red cabbage, carrot, red pepper, red onion and walnuts in a large bowl. Add dressing and toss to coat vegetables evenly. Season lightly with salt. Cover and chill thoroughly in the refrigerator.

To serve, mound onto salad plates, then garnish with chopped walnuts and chunks of blue cheese.

Beet Salad with Raspberry Vinaigrette and Goat Cheese

The beets that we use at Bishop's are grown for us by the King family on their Hazelmere Valley organic farm. We use both red and the less common golden beets. The reds usually weigh in at about 2 pounds/1 kg. We braise these big beets—they are never tough and are always really sweet. Gary King explains that it's best to leave root vegetables in the ground until they are fully grown, as this allows them to pick up all those great earthy flavours and, of course, more vitamins and minerals. Baby root vegetables look cute, but they just don't have the same full flavour or nutritional value.

Beet tops are also delicious. They can be added to a stir-fry, or steamed in a shallow pan in their own juices with a bit of garlic and ginger.

Here, the raspberry vinegar brings out the sweet flavour of the beets.

TO MAKE VINAIGRETTE Whisk together olive oil, raspberry vinegar and chopped basil. Season to taste with salt and pepper.

SALAD Cut tops off beets and wash them. Coarsely chop beet tops and set aside for garnish.

Place beets in a saucepan and add water to cover. Put the lid on the pot and boil on medium heat until tender when pierced with the point of a knife, 45 to 60 minutes. Drain and cool. Peel beets and cut into slices ¼ inch/ 6 mm thick.

To serve, arrange beet slices on salad plates. Drizzle with vinaigrette and top with crumbled goat (or feta) cheese. Garnish with a sprinkle of chopped beet tops around the edge.

½ cup	olive oil	125 mL
¼ cup	raspberry vinegar	60 mL
2	fresh basil leaves, chopped	2
	Salt and freshly ground black pepper	
2	medium-sized beets with tops on	2
½ cup	aged goat cheese or feta, crumbled	125 mL

4 servings

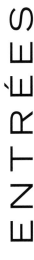

SPRING

Lamb Loin in Pastry with
Red Wine and Balsamic Sauce *72*

Honey Mustard Free-range
Chicken Breast *74*

Roasted Halibut with
Minted Pea Coulis *75*

Roasted Spring Salmon with
Rhubarb Compote *76*

Grilled Ahi Tuna with
Braised Greens and Warm Grainy
Mustard Vinaigrette *78*

Chardonnay-poached Prawns with
Lemon-Parsley Aïoli *79*

SUMMER

Roast Pork Tenderloin with
Savoury Sausage Stuffing *80*

Grilled Sockeye Salmon with
Charred Tomato Relish *81*

Pesto-crusted Halibut with
Red Lentil Dahl *83*

Split Roast Chicken with Pickled Peaches
and Garlic-roasted Potato Rounds *84*

Nova Scotia Lobster with
Ginger-Citrus Sabayon *86*

Poached Salmon in White Wine with
Fennel and Hand-peeled Shrimp *89*

Thick-cut Spice-rubbed Steak
with Red Wine Sauce and
Roasted Fingerling Potatoes *90*

AUTUMN

Grilled Beef Tenderloin with
Olive Oil–poached Yukon Gold
Potatoes and Blue Cheese *92*

Poached Halibut "T-bone" Steak with
Fresh Green Grapes *93*

Roast Chicken with Cornbread-Bacon
Pudding and Sherry Pan Gravy *94*

Braised Lamb Shanks with
Root Vegetables *96*

Grilled Quail with Roasted Corn
and Squash Curry *98*

Roast Turkey Breast with
Port Cranberry Compote *99*

Dungeness Crab Cakes with
Pear-Cranberry Chutney *100*

WINTER

Roast Duck Breast with Apple Purée *101*

Whole Roast Beef Tenderloin with Wild
Mushroom Ragout and Potato Gratin *102*

Slow-cooked Pork Shoulder with
Pan-roasted Vegetables *105*

Chicken Cassoulet *106*

Poached Halibut in Saffron-Tomato
Broth with Ruby Chard *108*

Grilled Prawns with Pumpkin Risotto *110*

Steamed Smoked Black Cod with
Herb-Horseradish Sabayon *111*

Lamb Loin in Pastry with
Red Wine and Balsamic Sauce

2	lamb racks (each 1.5 to 2 lb./ 700 to 900 g)	2
	Salt and freshly ground black pepper	
1	large onion, sliced	1
2	celery ribs, sliced	2
2	large carrots, sliced	2
1 cup	chopped Roma (plum) tomatoes	250 mL
1 cup	dry red wine	250 mL
½ cup	chopped fresh mint leaves	125 mL
4 cups	chicken stock	1 L
½ cup	balsamic vinegar	125 mL
8 oz.	frozen puff pastry, thawed	250 g
1 Tbsp.	Dijon mustard	15 mL
1	egg, beaten	1
	Fresh mint leaves for garnish	

4 to 6 servings

Trimming and deboning a rack of lamb does make for a bit of extra work, but the reward is that you can use the trim and bones to create a delicious sauce. And you can save time by buying frozen puff pastry instead of making your own.

The lamb can be made ahead and, once it has been wrapped in the pastry, can be kept covered and refrigerated for up to 24 hours prior to baking. The sauce can also be made ahead of time and then reheated when needed. Lamb cooked this way makes for a beautiful presentation when carved and plated. Serve with New Potatoes with Lemon and Parsley (page 114) and Balsamic and Honey Glazed Carrots (page 116).

TO MAKE To trim and debone a lamb rack, place on a cutting board in front of you, with the bone side facing up. Use a sharp boning or utility knife to cut the bones away from the meat of the rack. Pull the eye of the rack away from the cap of fat, leaving a nice loin of meat to use for the dish. Trim all the little bits of meat off the fat cap; discard the fat, but save all meat trim and bones to make sauce.

Season boneless lamb with salt and pepper. Heat a frying pan on high heat, then sear meat until browned on all sides, about 2 minutes per side. Set aside and allow to cool.

Heat a large heavy saucepan on medium-high heat, then brown meat trimmings and bones until they turn a deep brown colour, about 10 minutes. Add onion, celery and carrots; cook until vegetables are golden, about 10 minutes. Add tomatoes, red wine and mint, then bring to a simmer. Add chicken stock and bring to a boil. Turn down heat to low and simmer, uncovered, for 1 hour. Strain, add balsamic vinegar and return to the saucepan; continue simmering until reduced by two thirds, about 30 minutes. Keep sauce warm on a low-heat burner until needed.

Preheat the oven to 400°F/200°C and line a baking sheet with parchment paper.

Roll out puff pastry on a lightly floured surface to form a rectangle 8 by 12 inches/20 by 30 cm, to a thickness of ⅛ inch/3 mm. Cut in half to obtain two rectangles, each 6 by 8 inches/15 by 20 cm. Place one lamb loin in the centre of each pastry piece and brush meat with mustard. Then brush all around the edges of each pastry with beaten egg (reserving some to brush tops). Fold edges of each pastry over and press down to seal. Turn pastries over, seam side down, and brush tops with the remaining egg.

Place pastries on the prepared baking sheet and bake until pastry is golden, about 20 minutes. Remove from the oven and allow to rest for 10 minutes before carving.

To serve, cut each loin into slices ½ inch/1 cm thick. Ladle ¼ cup/60 mL of sauce onto each warmed plate and arrange meat slices on top of sauce. Garnish with mint leaves.

WINE Merlot or Shiraz

Honey Mustard Free-range Chicken Breast

½ cup	dry white wine	125 mL
¼ cup	honey	60 mL
½ cup	grainy mustard	125 mL
½ cup	vegetable oil	125 mL
	Pinch of freshly ground black pepper	
6	chicken breast halves or 1 whole cut-up chicken	6
	Sprigs of fresh thyme for garnish	

6 servings

Chef Dennis Green developed this marinade to cook the organic chickens that we get from local farmer Thomas Reid. We've found that organic or free-range chickens generally have much better flavour.

This amount of marinade makes enough for 6 chicken breast halves or 1 whole chicken cut into pieces. The marinade makes the chicken really tender while the honey makes the skin golden brown and crispy. This dish may be served warm or cold (perfect for a picnic).

Lining the baking pan with parchment paper will prevent the chicken from sticking as the marinade reduces and will make cleaning up much easier.

TO MAKE Combine white wine and honey in a small saucepan on medium heat and bring to a boil. Whisk in mustard, vegetable oil and pepper until well mixed, then allow to cool.

Place chicken in a shallow pan and pour marinade over it. Cover and marinate overnight in the refrigerator.

Preheat the oven to 400°F/200°C and line a shallow baking pan with parchment paper.

Remove chicken from marinade and place in the prepared baking pan. Bake until chicken is golden brown in colour and cooked, 20 to 30 minutes. Check for doneness with a meat thermometer; the internal temperature should read 175°F/80°C. Allow to rest for 5 minutes before serving.

To serve, either leave the chicken breasts (or cut-up pieces) whole or carve them diagonally and arrange slices on warmed plates. Garnish with a sprig of thyme.

WINE Red: Pinot Noir · White: Chardonnay

Roasted Halibut with Minted Pea Coulis

The word "roasting" conjures up images of large pieces of meat or poultry, and this is fine, but we chefs also love to roast seafood. We take thick cuts of fish and lightly pan-sear them to seal in the juices, then quickly roast them to keep the flesh moist and to retain the flavour.

Cooking halibut this way works well for dinner parties and for larger groups, because once the fish is on the tray and in the oven, you don't have to fuss with turning the fillets. Just serve from the roasting tray straight onto warmed plates.

TO MAKE COULIS Place shallot and white wine in a small saucepan on medium heat. Bring to a simmer and cook until liquid is reduced by half, about 5 minutes. Add peas, mint and whipping cream. Cook until peas are tender, about 5 minutes. Allow to cool for 10 to 15 minutes.

Purée in a blender or food processor and strain. Season to taste with salt. Transfer to a saucepan and set aside.

HALIBUT Preheat the oven to 400°F/200°C and line a baking sheet with parchment paper.

Season halibut with sea salt and pepper. Heat vegetable oil in a large ovenproof nonstick frying pan on high heat. Sear halibut on one side only until golden, about 2 to 3 minutes. Turn halibut over and transfer to the prepared baking sheet. Roast in the oven until halibut flesh is just opaque, about 5 minutes.

To serve, reheat pea coulis and ladle 2 to 3 Tbsp./30 to 45 mL onto each warmed plate. Place halibut on top of coulis and garnish with a curly pea top or sprig of parsley

WINE A dry Riesling or Pinot Blanc

COULIS

1	shallot, minced	1
¼ cup	dry white wine	60 mL
1 cup	fresh or frozen peas	250 mL
2 Tbsp.	chopped fresh mint leaves	30 mL
¼ cup	whipping cream	60 mL
	Salt	

HALIBUT

4	halibut fillets (each 6 oz./170 g)	4
	Sea salt and freshly ground black pepper	
1 Tbsp.	vegetable oil	15 mL
	Curly pea tops or fresh parsley for garnish	

4 servings

Roasted Spring Salmon with Rhubarb Compote

1½ cups	rice vinegar	375 mL
½ cup	sugar	125 mL
½	small red onion, ½-inch/1-cm dice	½
1 tsp.	grated fresh ginger	5 mL
1 lb.	rhubarb, 1-inch/ 2.5-cm thick slices	500 g
	Salt	

SALMON

4	spring salmon fillets (each 6 oz./170 g)	4
	Salt and freshly ground black pepper	

4 servings

I'm always thrilled whenever I cook the first fresh salmon of the year. Spring can still be a little too chilly for an outdoor barbecue, so roasting salmon fillets in the oven on parchment paper, the way we do in this recipe, is the next best thing. And, in fact, the salmon is a little easier to cook this way. The spicy, sweet and sour flavours of the rhubarb compote make a good sharp contrast to the richness of the salmon.

TO MAKE COMPOTE Combine rice vinegar and sugar in a saucepan on medium heat and bring to a simmer. Add onion, ginger and rhubarb. Cover and simmer until soft, about 45 minutes. Allow to cool for 10 to 15 minutes.

Purée in a blender or food processor. Season to taste with salt. Allow to cool and refrigerate in a covered container until needed. (Will keep for two weeks in the refrigerator.) Bring to room temperature before serving.

SALMON Preheat the oven to 400°F/200°C and line a baking sheet with parchment paper.

Season salmon with salt and pepper. Heat a nonstick frying pan on medium-high heat. Sear salmon on one side only until golden, 2 to 3 minutes.

Turn salmon over and transfer to the prepared baking sheet. Roast in the oven just until flesh in the centre is opaque, 5 to 7 minutes.

To serve, place a salmon fillet on each warmed plate and pour a ring of rhubarb compote around it.

WINE Red: Pinot Noir · White: Pinot Gris

Roasted spring salmon with rhubarb compote; grilled asparagus spears with raspberry-shallot vinaigrette (recipe page 115); potato, herb and onion latkes (recipe page 131) >

Grilled Ahi Tuna with Braised Greens and Warm Grainy Mustard Vinaigrette

VINAIGRETTE

½ cup	white wine vinegar	125 mL
1 cup	dry white wine	250 mL
1 Tbsp.	coarsely chopped shallot	15 mL
1 Tbsp.	honey	15 mL
2 Tbsp.	grainy mustard	30 mL
½ cup	olive oil	125 mL

TUNA WITH GREENS

1 Tbsp.	butter	15 mL
1 tsp.	minced garlic	5 mL
1 tsp.	grated fresh ginger	5 mL
1	bunch kale or Swiss chard, stems removed	1
	Sea salt and freshly ground black pepper	
4	Ahi tuna steaks (each 6 oz./170 g)	4
2 tsp.	vegetable oil	10 mL

4 servings

The secret to barbecuing tuna is to make sure the grill is clean, lightly oiled and at the proper temperature. Also, try to have the braised greens ready on warmed plates and the warm vinaigrette close by. That way, they'll be nice and hot and ready to serve as soon as the fish comes off the grill.

TO MAKE VINAIGRETTE Mix together white wine vinegar, white wine, shallot, honey and mustard in a small saucepan. Bring to a boil on medium heat, then simmer, uncovered, until liquid is reduced by half, 5 to 10 minutes. Allow to cool for 10 to 15 minutes.

Transfer to a blender or food processor and, with the motor running, gradually add olive oil until completely blended. Set aside and reheat when ready to serve.

TUNA WITH GREENS Preheat the barbecue or grill to high heat.

Melt butter in a frying pan on medium heat. Sauté garlic and ginger until aromatic, about 2 minutes. Add kale (or Swiss chard), then season with sea salt and pepper. (*Note:* The water left on the kale after washing will provide enough liquid for steaming.) Cover and cook until kale is tender, 2 to 3 minutes. Drain and keep warm.

Rub tuna steaks with vegetable oil, then season with sea salt and pepper. Grill to medium rare (fish will still feel soft to the touch), about 2 to 3 minutes per side. While fish is cooking, reheat vinaigrette.

To serve, place a mound of kale in the centre of each warmed plate and top with a tuna steak. Drizzle with vinaigrette.

WINE: White: Pinot Gris or Pinot Blanc · Red: lightly chilled Pinot Noir

Chardonnay-poached Prawns with Lemon-Parsley Aïoli

A steaming platter of seafood brought directly to the table always gets an enthusiastic reception. With this dish, I like to serve a bowl of simple cooked rice and steamed greens. I also suggest that you serve chilled glasses of the same type of Chardonnay in which you cooked the prawns. These prawns and their Lemon-Parsley Aïoli dip also make an excellent hors d'oeuvre.

Buying fresh seafood can be a challenge, even for us chefs who shop all the time, so try to get to know your fish supplier and ask for advice about which prawns are the freshest that day.

TO MAKE AÏOLI Place mayonnaise, lemon juice, garlic and parsley in a blender or food processor and process until smooth. Refrigerate in a covered container until needed. (Will keep in the refrigerator for 2 to 3 days.)

PRAWNS Combine olive oil, Chardonnay (or other white wine), water, lemon grass, shallot, thyme, bay leaf, peppercorns and sea salt in a soup pot. Bring to a simmer on medium-high heat. Add prawns, then bring back to a simmer. Cook, uncovered, until prawns turn pink, 3 to 4 minutes. Drain cooked prawns and arrange on a warmed serving platter.

To serve, put aïoli in a small bowl, then place the bowl in the middle of the prawn platter. Garnish with lemon wedges and sprigs of fresh thyme or parsley.

WINE Chardonnay

AÏOLI

1 cup	mayonnaise	250 mL
1	lemon, juiced	1
2	garlic cloves	2
1 Tbsp.	fresh parsley leaves	15 mL

PRAWNS

1 Tbsp.	olive oil	15 mL
1 cup	Chardonnay or other dry white wine	250 mL
1 cup	water	250 mL
1 Tbsp.	chopped lemon grass	15 mL
1	shallot, chopped	1
1	sprig fresh thyme	1
1	bay leaf	1
1 tsp.	whole black peppercorns	5 mL
1 tsp.	sea salt	5 mL
24	large prawn tails, peeled and deveined	24
	Lemon wedges for garnish	
	Sprigs of fresh thyme or parsley for garnish	

4 servings

Roast Pork Tenderloin with Savoury Sausage Stuffing

1½ lb.	pork tenderloin, in one piece	750 g
	Salt and freshly ground black pepper	
½ lb.	pork sausage meat	250 g
2 Tbsp.	finely chopped dried apricots	30 mL
1 Tbsp.	chopped fresh sage leaves	15 mL
1 Tbsp.	olive oil	15 mL
	Sprigs of fresh sage for garnish	

4 servings

With this savoury meat dish, I like to serve simple oven-roasted fruits such as apples or pears. Peel and core the fruit, then toss lightly with a shake or two of cinnamon, a little melted butter and a few drops of white wine. Roast the fruit beside the meat for the last 20 minutes of cooking and use for garnish.

TO MAKE Preheat the oven to 400°F/200°C.

Trim off and discard silver skin and any excess fat from pork. Use a sharp knife to butterfly the pork by making a long deep cut down the length of the tenderloin, being sure not to cut right through. Open up tenderloin and pound lightly to flatten. Season with salt and pepper.

Mix together sausage meat, dried apricots and sage in a bowl. Spread mixture inside butterflied tenderloin, then gently fold up to partially enclose stuffing. Use butcher twine to tie tenderloin closed in four places. Rub with olive oil, then season with salt and pepper.

Place tenderloin, cut side up, in a roasting pan and roast until done, about 45 minutes. Check for doneness with a meat thermometer; the internal temperature should read 160°F/70°C.

Allow meat to rest in a warm place, uncovered, for about 15 minutes before carving.

To serve, carve pork into slices 1 inch/2.5 cm thick and place on warmed plates. Garnish with sprigs of sage.

WINE Red: Chianti Classico · White: Pinot Grigio

Grilled Sockeye Salmon with Charred Tomato Relish

This charred tomato relish is one of the easiest and tastiest quick sauces I know of for a summer salmon barbecue. Sockeye is always our first choice for grilling because of its firm flesh and ability to stand up to the smoky flavours of the grill. Just be careful not to overcook this particular variety of salmon; otherwise, it can become dry.

TO MAKE RELISH Preheat the grill or barbecue on medium heat.

Place whole tomatoes on the grill and turn continually until well charred on all sides, 8 to 10 minutes. At the same time, grill onion slices until lightly charred on both sides, 5 to 6 minutes.

Coarsely chop grilled tomatoes and onions; place in a large bowl. Season well with sea salt and pepper. Toss with balsamic vinegar, olive oil and basil. Cover and let sit for 30 minutes at room temperature for flavours to develop.

Purée in a blender or food processor and strain through a coarse sieve. The relish can be served hot or cold. (Will keep in the refrigerator for a week.)

SALMON Preheat the grill or barbecue on high heat.

Rub salmon with vegetable oil, then season with sea salt and pepper. Grill until just cooked, 3 to 4 minutes per side.

To serve, place grilled salmon fillets on warmed plates and ladle 2 to 3 Tbsp./30 to 45 mL of relish on the side.

WINE White: a rich Pinot Gris · Red: Merlot or a lightly chilled Pinot Noir

RELISH

1 lb.	tomatoes (3 large)	500 g
1	small red onion, ¼-inch/6-mm thick slices	1
	Sea salt and freshly ground black pepper	
¼ cup	balsamic vinegar	60 mL
¼ cup	olive oil	60 mL
2	sprigs fresh basil	2

SALMON

4	sockeye salmon fillets (each 6 oz./170 g)	4
1 tsp.	vegetable oil	5 mL
	Sea salt and freshly ground black pepper	

4 servings

Pesto-crusted Halibut with Red Lentil Dahl

Recently, I visited India where meals included a lentil dahl, which tasted different each time, depending on who had cooked it. As soon as I arrived back home, I set to making the same kinds of lentil dishes for my family. The garam masala is a spice blend sold in Asian food stores.

TO MAKE DAHL Heat vegetable oil in a large saucepan on medium heat. Sauté onion, garlic and ginger until onion is soft, 4 to 5 minutes. Add lentils, garam masala, cumin and turmeric. (If you like your dahl a little spicier, add a dried whole chili pepper or two, then remove at the end of the cooking process.) Add water and bring to a simmer on medium-high heat, skimming off any foam that appears on the surface. Add sugar, salt and pepper. Cover and simmer for 45 minutes. (Lentil dahl can made ahead and will keep for 1 to 2 days in the refrigerator.)

PESTO Place basil, garlic, pine nuts, coarse salt and Parmesan cheese in a blender or food processor and grind into a paste. Slowly add extra-virgin olive oil until smooth. Refrigerate until needed. (Any extra pesto will keep for a week refrigerated, 3 months frozen.)

HALIBUT Preheat the oven to 400°F/200°C and line a baking sheet with parchment paper. Take 1 Tbsp./15 mL of pesto for each halibut fillet and rub in, then place fish on the prepared baking sheet. Bake until just cooked through so that flesh is opaque and firm to the touch, about 10 minutes.

To serve, reheat dahl and spoon onto warmed plates. Top each with a piece of halibut.

WINE Australian Semillon

< Pesto-crusted halibut with red lentil dahl

DAHL

2 Tbsp.	vegetable oil	30 mL
1	small onion, ¼-inch/ 6-mm dice	1
2	garlic cloves, crushed	2
1 Tbsp.	grated fresh ginger	15 mL
1 cup	red lentils	250 mL
½ tsp.	garam masala	2.5 mL
½ tsp.	cumin	2.5 mL
½ tsp.	turmeric	2.5 mL
4 cups	water	1 L
½ tsp.	sugar	2.5 mL
½ tsp.	salt	2.5 mL
	Freshly ground black pepper	

PESTO

½ lb.	fresh basil leaves	250 g
4	garlic cloves	4
2 Tbsp.	toasted pine nuts	30 mL
	Pinch of coarse salt	
½ cup	grated Parmesan cheese	125 mL
½ cup	extra-virgin olive oil	125 mL

HALIBUT

4	halibut fillets (each 6 oz./170 g)	4
	Salt and freshly ground black pepper	

4 servings

Split Roast Chicken with Pickled Peaches and Garlic Roasted Potato Rounds

6	large peaches	6
1 cup	apple cider vinegar	250 mL
1 cup	water	250 mL
½ cup	sugar	125 mL
1	cinnamon stick	1
6	whole allspice	6
	Pinch of ground cloves	

CHICKEN AND POTATOES

4	russet or other large potatoes	4
1	head garlic, cloves peeled	1
	Salt and freshly ground black pepper	
¼ cup	olive oil or vegetable oil	60 mL
1	chicken, split in half	1
1 Tbsp.	olive oil	15 mL
2	sprigs fresh thyme, chopped	2
1 tsp.	sweet paprika	5 mL
2 tsp.	salt, preferably coarse sea salt	10 mL

4 servings

This recipe is one of our slow-cook dishes that requires very little attention. The chicken is simply roasted without basting or turning. Try to buy free-range or organic chickens, as they really do taste so much better. The pickled peaches should be made ahead of time.

TO MAKE PEACHES Fill a bowl with ice-cold water. Next, bring a medium pot of water to a boil. Score peaches with a paring knife and place them in boiling water for 15 to 30 seconds, then plunge them into ice-cold water.

Using a paring knife, remove and discard skin from peaches. Run a knife down through the seam of the peach until you hit the stone. Turn the knife to remove the stone. Cut peaches into wedges ½ inch/1 cm thick at widest part and place in a bowl.

Combine apple cider vinegar, water, sugar, cinnamon stick, allspice and cloves in a saucepan and bring to a boil on medium-high heat. Pour over peaches and allow to cool. Cover and refrigerate to chill thoroughly before serving cold or at room temperature. (Will keep in the refrigerator for up to a week.)

CHICKEN AND POTATOES Preheat the oven to 375°F/190°C.

Peel potatoes and cut into rounds 1 inch/2.5 cm thick. Place potato rounds and garlic cloves in a roasting pan. Season with salt and pepper. Add ¼ cup/60 mL olive (or vegetable) oil and toss until potato rounds and garlic cloves are evenly coated. Lay potato rounds flat on the bottom of the roasting pan and surround them with garlic cloves.

Place chicken halves, skin side up, on top of potatoes. Brush chicken with 1 Tbsp./15 mL olive oil and season with thyme, sweet paprika and salt. Cover loosely with a sheet of aluminum foil, shiny side in, and place in the oven. Roast until done, about 2 hours. Check for doneness with a meat thermometer; the internal temperature should read 175°F/80°C. Remove chicken from the roasting pan and keep warm in a warming drawer or wrap in aluminum foil. Leave the oven on.

Place the roasting pan with potatoes and garlic back into the oven until potatoes brown a bit more, about 15 minutes.

To serve, place 2 to 3 potato rounds on each warmed plate. Carve chicken and arrange slices on plates, making sure each serving has an equal amount of light and dark meat. Serve pickled peaches in a dish on the side.

WINE A spicy Gewürztraminer or Viognier

Nova Scotia Lobster with Ginger-Citrus Sabayon

SABAYON

½ cup	mixed citrus juices (orange, lemon, lime)	125 mL
1 tsp.	grated fresh ginger	5 mL
2	egg yolks	2
½ cup	butter, softened	125 mL
	Salt and freshly ground black pepper	

LOBSTER

2	lobsters (each 1½ lb./750 g)	2
1 tsp.	butter, melted	5 mL

4 servings

This recipe takes beautiful, fresh Atlantic lobster and prepares it in two different ways: we roast the tail and boil the claws. Everyone at the table will have fun opening the shells and dipping the lobster meat into the sabayon.

If you prefer to use spiny lobster (either the Pacific or Caribbean variety), you won't have the claws. Be sure to freeze the heads to make shellfish stock (page 164) or bisque.

TO MAKE SABAYON Combine citrus juices, ginger, and egg yolks in a stainless steel bowl. Place the bowl over hot but not simmering water in a saucepan on medium heat.

Whisk mixture together until it is pale and slightly thickened. Whisk in butter 1 Tbsp./15 mL at a time until it is all incorporated. Season to taste with salt and pepper. Remove from the heat and cover loosely with a clean cloth to keep warm until needed.

LOBSTER Preheat the oven to 400°F/200°C and bring a saucepan of salted water to a boil.

To kill lobster, place it on a cutting board and insert a sharp knife into the centre of the head, between the eyes. Remove the claws by twisting them off.

Use a pair of kitchen shears to cut the shell of the lobster tail in half down the centre of both sides. Use a sharp knife to cut tail meat in half and rinse to remove spinal cord.

Brush each half tail with melted butter and place them on a baking sheet. Roast in the oven until meat changes colour to bright pink, 5 to 8 minutes.

At the same time, place lobster claws in the pot of boiling water on high heat. Simmer, uncovered, until they change colour to bright pink, about 8 minutes; drain. Use a pair of lobster crackers or the back of a heavy chef's knife to crack the shells of the cooked claws to make it easier for your guests.

To serve, place a half tail and a cracked claw on each warmed plate, with small individual ramekins of warm sabayon for dipping.

WINE A rich Chardonnay or Pinot Gris

Poached Salmon in White Wine with Fennel and Hand-peeled Shrimp

I like to make this elegant midsummer dish using wild spring salmon, which is in season at that time. I prefer to use white pepper for the sauce, as it is subtler and much milder in flavour than black pepper.

Use a sharp vegetable or potato peeler to remove the sometimes tough exterior of the fennel bulb.

TO MAKE Remove and discard the skin and any pin bones from salmon. Also remove and discard any dark meat that remains after removing the skin. Cut fillet into four pieces.

Place salmon pieces in a large frying pan. Pour in white wine, cover, and bring to a simmer on medium-high heat. Turn down the heat to low and poach salmon until it turns white in colour and is cooked, about 5 minutes. Use a slotted lifter to transfer salmon to a warmed plate and cover to keep warm while you make the sauce; keep the poaching liquid in the pan.

Return the frying pan and poaching liquid back to the stove on medium-high heat and bring to a simmer. Add fennel, shallot, tomato, garlic, whipping cream and shrimp. Turn down the heat to medium-low and simmer, uncovered, until vegetables are tender, about 10 minutes. Season to taste with salt and white pepper.

To serve, place a piece of salmon on each warmed dinner plate. Pour a ladle of sauce over each piece of salmon and garnish with chopped fennel top.

WINE A rich Riesling

1 lb.	boneless salmon fillet	500 g
2 cups	dry white wine	500 mL
1 cup	thinly sliced fennel bulb	250 mL
1 Tbsp.	finely chopped shallot	15 mL
1	tomato, peeled, seeded, ¼-inch/6-mm dice	1
1	garlic clove, minced	1
1 cup	whipping cream	250 mL
½ lb.	fresh hand-peeled baby shrimp	250 g
	Salt and white pepper	
1 tsp.	chopped fennel top, for garnish	5 mL

4 servings

< Nova Scotia lobster with ginger-citrus sabayon (recipe page 86); lobster and saffron risotto (recipe page 120)

Thick-cut Spice-rubbed New York Steak with Red Wine Sauce and Roasted Fingerling Potatoes

1 Tbsp.	black peppercorns	15 mL
1 tsp.	pink or green peppercorns	5 mL
1 tsp.	dill seeds	5 mL
1 tsp.	fennel seeds	5 mL
1 tsp.	coriander seeds	5 mL
1 tsp.	Szechuan pepper	5 mL
1 tsp.	yellow mustard seeds	5 mL
1 tsp.	brown mustard seeds	5 mL
½ tsp.	chili flakes	2.5 mL

SAUCE (OPTIONAL)

2 Tbsp.	vegetable oil	30 mL
2	shallots, chopped	2
2	garlic cloves, chopped	2
1 cup	mushrooms, sliced	250 mL
½ cup	dry red wine	125 mL
1 Tbsp.	tomato paste	15 mL
1 Tbsp.	Worcestershire sauce	15 mL
4 cups	chicken stock	1 L
	Salt and freshly ground black pepper	

A thick-cut New York or rib eye steak is a family favourite at our house. I get the butcher to cut it 2 inches/5 cm thick because I like to carve my steaks; I think this makes for a better presentation on the plate and also makes the meat go further.

The spice rub recipe is a blend of peppery and sweet that makes a delicious crust on any grilled or roasted meat or poultry. Marinating adds a lot more flavour and also acts as a tenderizer. This marinade can also be used for poultry and pork.

I sometimes think potatoes are the best part of any meal. Fingerling potatoes, which are fairly new to markets, taste delicious when roasted whole. They can also simply be steamed and used to make a potato salad. If you are unable to find fingerlings, use baby red potatoes instead.

TO MAKE SPICE RUB Combine all spice rub ingredients and finely grind, using a pestle and mortar or an electric spice mill. (Store any leftover spice rub in an air-tight jar—it keeps indefinitely and can also be used to season chicken or pork.)

SAUCE (OPTIONAL) Heat vegetable oil in a saucepan on medium-high heat. Sauté shallots, garlic and mushrooms until tender, 5 to 10 minutes.

Deglaze the pan by adding red wine and stirring to loosen the browned bits on the bottom. Add tomato paste, Worcestershire sauce and stock. Bring to a boil, then turn down heat to low; simmer, uncovered, until reduced by half, about 40 minutes. Remove from the heat and allow to cool for 15 minutes.

Purée in a blender or food processor. Season to taste with salt and pepper. Reheat before serving. (Sauce can be made ahead and kept stored in the refrigerator for 3 to 4 days.)

STEAK In a stainless steel, glass or ceramic container large enough to contain the steak, mix together vegetable oil, garlic, rosemary, thyme and soy sauce (optional).

Trim off and discard any excess fat from steak. Cut steak crosswise into two thick pieces and place them in the marinade, making sure they are completely covered with oil. Tightly seal the container with plastic wrap and refrigerate overnight or up to 3 days. Turn steaks occasionally to make sure marinade permeates them evenly.

POTATOES Preheat the oven to 375°F/190°C.

Toss together potatoes, vegetable oil, garlic and sea salt in a large roasting pan. Bake in the oven until potatoes are golden in colour and tender when pricked with a fork, about 45 minutes.

TO COOK STEAK While potatoes are cooking, preheat the barbecue or grill pan on high heat.

Remove steaks from marinade, pat off any excess and season with spice rub. Grill until desired doneness: 4 to 5 minutes on each side for rare, 7 to 8 minutes on each side for medium. Transfer steaks to a cooler part of the grill or a warming drawer and keep warm, uncovered, for 10 to 15 minutes, to rest before carving.

To serve, carve steaks and arrange slices in the centre of warmed plates. Place fingerling potatoes alongside. Reheat sauce (optional) and pour around edge of plates.

WINE A hearty red from Chile or Argentina

STEAK

2 cups	vegetable oil	500 mL
4	garlic cloves	4
1	sprig fresh rosemary	1
2	sprigs fresh thyme	2
1 Tbsp.	soy sauce (optional)	15 mL
1½ lb.	New York steak in one piece (2 inches/ 5 cm thick)	750 g
1 Tbsp.	spice rub	15 mL

POTATOES

16	fingerling potatoes, cut in half	16
2 Tbsp.	vegetable oil	30 mL
2	garlic cloves, coarsely chopped	2
1 tsp.	sea salt	5 mL

4 servings

Grilled Beef Tenderloin with Olive Oil–poached Yukon Gold Potatoes and Blue Cheese

POTATOES

2 cups	olive oil	500 mL
½ cup	onion, 1-inch/ 2.5-cm dice	125 mL
1	sprig fresh rosemary	1
6	medium potatoes, peeled, 1-inch/ 2.5-cm dice	6
	Salt and freshly ground black pepper	

STEAK

4	beef tenderloin steaks or filet mignon (each 6 oz./170 g)	4
	Sea salt and freshly ground pepper	
2 oz.	your favourite blue cheese	60 g

4 servings

Beef tenderloin is a little more expensive than other cuts, but it is very lean and always tender. The first time I made these poached potatoes, I used up our entire home supply of extra-virgin olive oil. Nowadays, I buy a slightly less expensive olive oil to cook them in, and they are still very tasty. I prefer to use Yukon Gold potatoes to make this dish.

TO MAKE POTATOES Heat 2 Tbsp./30 mL of the olive oil until warm in a large saucepan on medium heat. Add onion and sauté until slightly softened, 3 to 4 minutes. Add rosemary, potatoes and remaining olive oil. Season with salt and pepper. Turn down heat to low and cook, uncovered, until potatoes are tender, about 45 minutes. (While the potatoes are cooking, grill the steaks.)

Remove and discard rosemary. Raise the heat to medium-high for 3 to 5 minutes to brown potatoes. Strain. Discard the used oil.

STEAK Preheat the barbecue or grill on medium-high heat.

Season steaks with sea salt and pepper. Grill until desired doneness: 3 to 4 minutes on each side for rare, 6 to 7 minutes on each side for medium. Remove from the heat and keep warm, uncovered, in a cooler part of the grill or in a warming drawer for 5 to 10 minutes, to allow the meat to rest.

To serve, place each steak on a warmed plate, along with a spoonful of poached potatoes. Top each steak with a piece of blue cheese.

WINE Cabernet Sauvignon or Merlot

Poached Halibut "T-bone" Steak with Fresh Green Grapes

Fresh halibut cooked on the bone is delicious; just make sure you carefully remove all the bones before serving. The sauce is easy to prepare and the ripe green grapes not only make a very pretty garnish but their natural acidity cuts through the richness of the cream in the sauce.

TO MAKE Place halibut steaks in a shallow frying pan and cover them with white vermouth. Bring to a simmer on medium heat; cook, uncovered, until flesh is just opaque, 5 to 8 minutes. Use a slotted lifter to carefully transfer fish to a platter and keep warm in a low-temperature oven or a warming drawer. Reserve the frying pan and vermouth.

Combine whipping cream and egg yolks in a small bowl, then whisk mixture into the vermouth. Bring back up to a simmer on medium heat, but do not boil. Simmer, uncovered, for 2 to 3 minutes. Season with sea salt and white pepper to taste. Add grapes at the last minute before serving.

To serve, remove all of the pin bones and centre bones from halibut steaks, then place them on warmed plates. Gently coat each halibut steak with the now silky grape sauce and garnish with finely chopped chives.

WINE Chenin Blanc

4	halibut steaks, on the bone (each 6 oz./170 g)	4
2 cups	white vermouth	500 mL
½ cup	whipping cream	125 mL
2	egg yolks	2
	Sea salt and white pepper	
½ cup	fresh green grapes, halved and deseeded	125 mL
	Finely chopped fresh chives for garnish	

4 servings

Roast Chicken with Cornbread-Bacon Pudding and Sherry Pan Gravy

1 tsp.	olive oil	5 mL
½ cup	red onion, ¼-inch/ 6-mm dice	125 mL
¼ cup	bacon, ¼-inch/ 6-mm dice	60 mL
½ cup	fresh corn kernels	125 mL
2 Tbsp.	chopped fresh parsley	30 mL
2 Tbsp.	chopped fresh thyme	30 mL
2 Tbsp.	chopped fresh chives	30 mL
1½ cups	crumbled day-old cornbread	375 mL
2	eggs	2
1 cup	milk	250 mL

This chicken dish can also make a small but perfect meal for Thanksgiving or some other festive occasion. Serve it with roasted squash and steamed green vegetables.

TO MAKE PUDDING Preheat the oven to 350°F/175°C. Butter a loaf pan 8½ × 4½ inches/21.5 × 11.5 cm; or 4 ramekins, each 4 oz./125 mL.

Heat olive oil in a frying pan on medium heat and sauté red onion until tender, 2 to 3 minutes. Add bacon and sauté until it begins to brown, 2 to 3 minutes. Drain bacon mixture and place in a bowl; stir in corn, parsley, thyme, chives and cornbread.

In a separate bowl, whisk together eggs and milk; stir into cornbread mixture.

Pour pudding mixture into the prepared loaf pan (or ramekins) and set in a baking pan. Place the pan on the middle shelf of the oven and fill halfway up to the top of loaf pan (or ramekins) with boiling water. Bake until pudding is done, 25 to 30 minutes. Test for doneness by placing a toothpick into the centre of the pudding(s). If it feels warm on your lips, pudding is cooked. Carefully remove the baking pan from the oven and let the loaf pan (or ramekins) cool in the water.

CHICKEN Preheat the oven to 450°F/230°C.

Season chicken breasts with salt and pepper, then dredge in flour, knocking off excess. Heat vegetable oil in a large ovenproof frying pan on medium-high heat. Sear chicken, skin side down, for 3 to 4 minutes. Turn chicken over, then place the pan in the oven and roast, skin side up, until cooked and juices run clear when a knife is inserted in the thickest part, 20 to 25 minutes.

Transfer chicken to a platter and keep warm in a warming drawer or a low-temperature oven (reserve roasting pan and drippings).

To make gravy, add flour to drippings in the roasting pan on medium heat, whisking until well combined. Deglaze the pan by adding sherry and stirring to loosen the browned bits on the bottom. Add stock and simmer, uncovered, for 15 to 20 minutes. Strain.

To serve, unmold cornbread-bacon pudding and cut into slices ½ inch/1 cm thick. (If made in ramekins, unmold and leave whole.) Place pudding on warmed plates, then carefully take chicken off the bone and place on top of the cornbread. Ladle some gravy over the chicken.

WINE Red: a lightly chilled Beaujolais · White: Chardonnay or white Burgundy

CHICKEN AND GRAVY

4	large chicken breast halves, bone in	4
	Salt and freshly ground black pepper	
	Flour for dredging	
¼ cup	vegetable oil	60 mL
1 Tbsp.	flour	15 mL
¼ cup	dry sherry	60 mL
2 cups	chicken stock	500 mL

4 servings

Braised Lamb Shanks with Root Vegetables

4	lamb shanks	4
	Salt and freshly ground black pepper	
	Flour for dusting	
¼ cup	vegetable oil	60 mL
1	large onion, ½-inch/ 1-cm dice	1
4	garlic cloves, chopped	4
½ cup	carrots, ½-inch/ 1-cm dice	125 mL
½ cup	celery root, ½-inch/ 1-cm dice	125 mL
½ cup	turnip, ½-inch/ 1-cm dice	125 mL
½ cup	parsnips, ½-inch/ 1-cm dice	125 mL
1 cup	dry red wine	250 mL
1	can Roma (plum) tomatoes, chopped (28 oz./796 mL)	1
3	cups chicken stock	750 mL
1	sprig fresh rosemary	1

4 servings

Lamb shanks are perfect for this slow-cooked comfort-food dish, and they are less expensive than veal shanks. The vegetables are cooked right in the dish, so all you have to do is serve a simple starch with them, such as steamed or mashed potatoes, or hot crusty bread. This dish is at its best made a day ahead to allow the flavours time to develop, then reheated to serve.

TO MAKE Preheat the oven to 375°F/190°C.

Trim off and discard any excess fat or gristle from lamb shanks. Season with salt and pepper, then dust with flour. Heat vegetable oil in a large frying pan on medium-high heat and sear lamb until golden brown on all sides, about 10 minutes. Transfer to a casserole dish, but reserve the pan and its drippings.

Place onion, garlic, carrots, celery root, turnip and parsnips in the same pan in which you browned the lamb and sauté until lightly browned, 4 to 5 minutes.

Deglaze the pan by adding red wine and stirring to loosen the browned bits on the bottom. Add tomatoes, stock and rosemary. Heat to a simmer, then pour mixture over lamb shanks.

Cover casserole dish with a tight-fitting lid or aluminum foil and bake until meat is tender, about 2½ hours.

To serve, place a shank on each warmed plate, arrange some vegetables on the side, and pour some of the braising liquid over top.

WINE A simple rustic red from southern France or Italy

Braised lamb shanks with root vegetables >

Grilled Quail with Roasted Corn and Squash Curry

2	ears corn	2
2 Tbsp.	olive oil	30 mL
½ cup	onion, ¼-inch/6-mm dice	125 mL
½ cup	acorn squash, ¼-inch/6-mm dice	125 mL
½ cup	green zucchini, ¼-inch/6-mm dice	125 mL
½ cup	yellow zucchini, ¼-inch/6-mm dice	125 mL
1 tsp.	curry powder	5 mL
1 tsp.	ground cumin	5 mL
1 tsp.	sweet paprika	5 mL
½ cup	dry sherry	125 mL
1	can coconut milk (14 oz./398 mL)	1
½ cup	whipping cream	125 mL
	Salt and freshly ground black pepper	

QUAIL

8	quail	8
¼ cup	vegetable oil	60 mL
1	orange, zest and juice	1
1 Tbsp.	chopped fresh thyme	15 mL
	Salt and freshly ground black pepper	

4 servings

You can make this curry, so redolent of autumn, ahead of time, and then reheat it; in fact, it will improve in flavour if you do. It's perfect with the grilled quail.

TO MAKE CURRY Husk and rinse ears of corn. Heat a non-stick pan or grill pan on medium-high heat. Add corn and dry roast, turning so it cooks on all sides, for 3 to 4 minutes. Use a sharp knife to cut kernels off the cobs.

Heat olive oil in a saucepan on medium heat. Sauté onion, squash, and green and yellow zucchini until onion is soft, 3 to 4 minutes. Add curry powder, cumin, paprika and corn kernels; sauté for a further 2 to 3 minutes.

Deglaze the pan by adding sherry and stirring to loosen the browned bits on the bottom. Stir in coconut milk and whipping cream. Turn down the heat to low and simmer, uncovered, until liquid is slightly thickened, about 15 minutes. Season to taste with salt and pepper. Cover and keep warm on low heat.

QUAIL Use a pair of poultry shears or the point of a sharp chef's knife to butterfly quail by cutting through the backbone. Press down to flatten. Place quail in a dish large enough to hold them all. Whisk together vegetable oil, orange zest and juice, thyme, salt and pepper in a bowl; pour over quail. Cover and place in the refrigerator to marinate for 1 hour.

Preheat the grill or barbecue on medium heat.

Remove quail from marinade and shake off excess. Grill until done, 5 minutes on each side.

To serve, spoon curry onto warmed plates and top each serving with 2 quail.

WINE Gewürztraminer or Riesling

For meals on Easter, Thanksgiving and Christmas or other special days, it's great to go all out, especially when entertaining a large group of family and friends. That's when we cook the whole bird; but for the times when there's just us and the cats, we often buy a smaller cut such as a boneless free-range breast of turkey. This will make a dinner for up to five people with lots of lean white meat for everybody, and there is no big bird to cook and carve. Instead of gravy, I serve this rich and spicy make-ahead fruit compote with a large bowl of creamy mashed potatoes and Oven-braised Celery (page 135). Yum!

TO MAKE COMPOTE Combine cranberries, port, orange zest and juice, ginger, sugar and water in a saucepan and bring to a boil on medium-high heat. Reduce the heat to low and simmer, uncovered, for 20 minutes. Allow to cool and refrigerate to chill well before serving. Can be made ahead of time. (Will keep refrigerated for 2 weeks.)

TURKEY Preheat the oven to 400°F/200°C.

Place turkey breast in a roasting pan and rub with vegetable (or olive) oil, then season with sea salt and pepper. Roast in the oven for about 45 minutes, until turkey registers an internal temperature of 170°F/75°C on a meat thermometer. Transfer turkey to a warmed platter and allow to rest for 10 minutes before carving.

To serve, carve turkey breast into thin slices and arrange them on warmed plates. Spoon cranberry compote on top.

WINE Red: Barolo · White: a dry Muscat or Gewürztraminer

COMPOTE

2 cups	cranberries	500 mL
½ cup	non-vintage port	125 mL
2	oranges, zest and juice	2
1 tsp.	grated fresh ginger	5 mL
½ cup	sugar	125 mL
½ cup	water	125 mL

TURKEY

2 lb.	turkey breast half, boneless	1 kg
2 Tbsp.	vegetable or olive oil	30 mL
	Sea salt and freshly ground black pepper	

4 to 5 servings

Dungeness Crab Cakes with Pear-Cranberry Chutney

CHUTNEY

1	small red onion, ¼-inch/6-mm dice	1
½ cup	sugar	125 mL
1 cup	apple cider vinegar	250 mL
1 Tbsp.	grated fresh ginger	15 mL
1	garlic clove, minced	1
4	pears, peeled, cored, ½-inch/1-cm dice	4
1 cup	dried cranberries	250 mL
1	cinnamon stick	1

CRAB CAKES

½ cup	cornmeal	125 mL
1 cup	coarse fresh bread crumbs	250 mL
1 lb.	cooked Dungeness crabmeat	500 g
1	egg	1
½ cup	mayonnaise	125 mL
2 Tbsp.	chopped green onion	30 mL
2 Tbsp.	chopped fresh parsley	30 mL
2 Tbsp.	chopped fresh basil	30 mL
1	lemon, zest and juice	1
	Salt and freshly ground black pepper	
½ cup	vegetable oil	125 mL
	Young salad greens for garnish	

4 servings

The secret to making crab cakes is to use lots of crabmeat and not too much bread filling. You can make this chutney with different kinds of fruit, depending on what is in season. In the spring, rhubarb is delicious, and so are ripe plums in the summer. The chutney also goes well with grilled meats such as chicken or lamb and can be made well in advance of the meal and stored in a covered container in the refrigerator for several weeks, just like jam.

TO MAKE CHUTNEY Combine onion, sugar, apple cider vinegar, ginger and garlic in a saucepan. Bring to a boil on medium-high heat, then add pears, dried cranberries and cinnamon stick. Turn down heat to medium and simmer, covered, until fruit is tender, about 25 minutes. Cool, then remove and discard cinnamon stick. Serve at room temperature. (Will keep in the refrigerator for several weeks.)

CRAB CAKES To make breading, place cornmeal and ½ cup of the bread crumbs in a blender or food processor and mix well until crumbs are fine.

Combine remaining bread crumbs, crabmeat, egg, mayonnaise, green onion, parsley, basil, lemon zest and juice in a bowl. Season with salt and pepper. Shape mixture into 8 rounds, 1 inch/2.5 cm thick and 2 to 3 inches/5 to 7.5 cm in diameter. Coat all over with cornmeal breading.

Heat vegetable oil in a large frying pan on medium-high heat. Fry crab cakes until golden and warmed through, about 5 minutes per side.

To serve, place two crab cakes on each warmed plate. Top each crab cake with a small spoon of chutney. Garnish the rims of the plates with an assortment of young salad greens.

WINE Sauvignon Blanc or Chardonnay

Roast Duck Breast with Apple Purée

Duck breasts are almost impossible to buy by themselves, so I buy the birds whole, and then remove the breasts and legs. I freeze the carcasses to make stock from later, and freeze the legs for a duck stew with turnips. The duck legs could also be used in place of chicken in the Chicken Cassoulet (page 106).

TO MAKE PURÉE Melt butter in a frying pan on medium heat. Sauté apple and shallots until lightly browned, about 5 minutes. Add apple cider vinegar and maple syrup; simmer, uncovered, until reduced by half, 5 to 7 minutes. Add stock and continue simmering, uncovered, until reduced by half, another 5 to 7 minutes. Allow to cool for a few minutes.

Transfer to a blender or food processor and purée, adding chilled butter 1 Tbsp./15 mL at a time. Season to taste with salt (optional). Keep warm in a covered saucepan on low heat.

DUCK Preheat the oven to 450°F/230°C.

Score the fat on duck breasts in a cross-hatch pattern ⅛-inch/3-mm deep to help render the fat while cooking. Season duck with salt and pepper. Heat an ovenproof frying pan on medium heat. Sear duck, skin side down, until lightly browned, about 5 minutes. Turn over and sear lightly on the other side, about 3 minutes.

Turn over again, so duck is skin side down. Place pan in the oven and roast until duck is medium rare, 5 to 8 minutes. Remove from the oven and allow to rest for 5 minutes.

To serve, carve duck into thin slices on a bias. Ladle a pool of apple purée onto each warmed plate and arrange duck slices on top.

WINE Red: Pinot Noir · White: Riesling

PURÉE

2 Tbsp.	butter	30 mL
1	apple, peeled, cored and quartered	1
2	shallots, sliced	2
½ cup	apple cider vinegar	125 mL
2 Tbsp.	maple syrup	30 mL
1 cup	chicken stock	250 mL
½ cup	chilled butter	125 mL
	Salt (optional)	

DUCK

4	duck breast halves	4
	Salt and freshly ground black pepper	

4 servings

Whole Roast Beef Tenderloin with
Wild Mushroom Ragout and Potato Gratin

POTATO GRATIN

6	large russet potatoes	6
1 Tbsp.	butter	15 mL
½ cup	sliced shallots	125 mL
¼ cup	olive oil	60 mL
	Salt and freshly ground black pepper	
1 Tbsp.	chopped fresh thyme	15 mL
1 Tbsp.	chopped fresh rosemary	15 mL

This beef tenderloin is perfect for a large dinner party or for carving at a buffet table. Roasting it whole like this and keeping the meat rare (but making sure to let it rest) will ensure a lovely pink colour when the tenderloin is carved.

The potato gratin has lots of good flavour and texture, and is a simple yet sophisticated variation on scalloped potatoes; the layers of very thinly sliced potatoes are held together with a little olive oil and some herbs.

Put the beef into the oven 15 to 30 minutes after you put in the Potato Gratin, so that everything is ready at the same time.

TO MAKE POTATOES Preheat the oven to 400°F/200°C and line a baking sheet with parchment paper.

Peel potatoes and cut lengthwise into slices ¹⁄₁₆ inch/ 2 mm thick.

Melt butter in a frying pan on medium heat. Sauté shallots until tender and golden, 5 to 6 minutes.

Brush the parchment paper on the baking sheet with a little of the olive oil and arrange a layer of potatoes, overlapping slices, to cover the paper. Brush potatoes with a little olive oil, season with salt and pepper and sprinkle with half of the shallots, half of the thyme and half of the rosemary.

Repeat the process for a second layer of potatoes, olive oil, shallots, thyme, rosemary, salt and pepper. Top with the remaining potatoes and brush with olive oil. Cover with a second sheet of parchment paper and a second baking sheet, to help keep potatoes flat while they cook.

Place potatoes in the oven. (Place beef in the oven 15 to 30 minutes after putting in potatoes.) Bake potatoes until tender, 45 to 60 minutes. Remove from the oven and allow to cool slightly, then cut into 4-inch/10-cm squares.

TENDERLOIN Brush beef with vegetable oil, then season with sea salt and pepper. Heat a frying pan on high heat, then sear beef on all sides, about 10 minutes. Transfer to a roasting pan.

Roast beef for 25 to 30 minutes. Check for doneness with a meat thermometer; the internal temperature should read 125°F/50°C. Remove from the oven and allow to rest for 15 minutes before carving.

RAGOUT While beef is resting and potatoes are cooling, make the ragout. Melt butter in a frying pan on medium heat. Sauté shallots and garlic until softened, 2 to 3 minutes. Add mushrooms and sauté until golden, 5 to 6 minutes.

Deglaze the pan by adding sherry and stirring to loosen the browned bits on the bottom. Add stock, thyme and rosemary, then simmer, uncovered, until liquid is reduced by three quarters, about 15 minutes.

To serve, carve beef into slices 1½ inches/4 cm thick, one per serving. Place a potato square on each warmed plate, then lay a slice of beef up against the potato. Spoon the ragout around the plate.

WINE An aged Cabernet Sauvignon

TENDERLOIN

3 lb.	centre-cut beef tenderloin in one piece	1.5 kg
1 Tbsp.	vegetable oil	15 mL
	Sea salt and freshly ground black pepper	

RAGOUT

2 Tbsp.	butter	30 mL
2	shallots, sliced	2
1	garlic clove, minced	1
½ lb.	wild mushrooms, sliced	250 g
½ cup	dry sherry	125 mL
½ cup	chicken stock	125 mL
1 tsp.	chopped fresh thyme	5 mL
1 tsp.	chopped fresh rosemary	5 mL

6 to 8 servings

Slow-cooked Pork Shoulder with Pan-roasted Vegetables

Slow-cooked meat is such a delight. Once it's in the oven, you can forget about it for a few hours, and the meat becomes so tender that it just pulls away from the bone. Shoulder cuts are best for slow-cooking recipes because they require longer cooking times and have lots of flavour— a bonus with such an economical cut of meat.

TO MAKE Preheat the oven to 450°F/230°C.

Grind together sea salt, brown sugar, fennel, coriander, mustard seeds and peppercorns with a mortar and pestle or in an electric spice mill. Rub meat with olive oil and ground spices.

Combine onions, carrots, parsnips and turnip in a roasting pan. Place pork shoulder on top of vegetables. Roast in the oven until meat is well coloured, about 45 minutes. Cover tightly with aluminum foil, shiny side in, and turn down the oven to 350°F/175°C. Roast until meat is fully cooked and pulls away from the bone, about 3 hours.

Transfer meat to a warmed platter and allow to rest for 15 to 20 minutes. Strain liquid from vegetables, then skim and discard fat from the surface; return liquid back to vegetables.

To serve, carve slices of pork and serve with vegetables on the side.

WINE Red: Pinot Noir · White: a medium-dry Riesling

1 Tbsp.	sea salt	15 mL
1 tsp.	brown sugar	5 mL
1 tsp.	fennel seeds	5 mL
1 tsp.	coriander seeds	5 mL
1 tsp.	mustard seeds	5 mL
1 tsp.	black peppercorns	5 mL
3½ lb.	bonelss pork shoulder, rolled and tied	1.5 kg
2 Tbsp.	olive oil	30 mL
1 cup	onions, 1-inch/ 2.5-cm dice	250 mL
2 cups	carrots, 1-inch/ 2.5-cm dice	500 mL
1 cup	parsnips, 1-inch/ 2.5-cm dice	250 mL
1 cup	turnip, 1-inch/ 2.5-cm dice	250 mL

4 servings

< Whole roast beef tenderloin with wild mushroom
ragout and potato gratin (recipe page 103);
oven-braised celery (recipe page 135)

Chicken Cassoulet

1 cup	dried white beans	250 mL
2 Tbsp.	olive oil	30 mL
6	skinless boneless chicken thighs, 1½-inch/4-cm cubes	6
1	onion, ½-inch/1-cm dice	1
3	carrots, peeled, ½-inch/1-cm dice	3
1 cup	rutabaga, peeled, ½-inch/1-cm dice	250 mL
1 cup	fennel bulb, peeled, ½-inch/1-cm dice	250 mL
2	celery ribs, ½-inch/1-cm dice	2
1	medium potato, peeled, ½-inch/1-cm dice	1
6	garlic cloves, chopped	6
1 Tbsp.	tomato paste	15 mL
½ cup	dry white wine	125 mL
1	large sprig fresh rosemary	1
1	sprig fresh thyme	1
1	bay leaf	1
2	cloves pressed into a small piece of onion	2
4	cups chicken stock	1 L
	Salt and freshly ground black pepper	

This dish is classic French comfort food: country cooking that is so simple and practical. For this recipe, I love to use my large Hornby Island pottery casserole. It has a big heavy lid that seals in all the slow-cooking juices, and when the cassoulet is finally ready, the pot can go right onto the centre of the table. Just make sure you protect your table top with a wooden chopping board or trivet.

The essential ingredients are white beans, root vegetables, meat of some form (in this version we use chicken, preferably free-range), lots of garlic and lots of lovely herb flavours, with a crispy buttered bread crumb topping. This is the kind of dish that you put in the oven in the afternoon—then you are free to go do whatever you like for a couple of hours. When you come back, just add the topping and brown it in the oven. Serve with lightly steamed green vegetables such as Swiss chard or French beans.

TO MAKE CASSOULET Place beans in a bowl, add enough cold water to cover them and soak overnight. (Alternatively, place beans in a saucepan, cover with cold water and bring slowly to a boil. Simmer, uncovered, on medium heat, for 5 minutes, then remove the pot from the burner and cover. Let stand while you prepare chicken, vegetables and topping.)

Preheat the oven to 300°F/150°C.

Heat olive oil in a frying pan on medium heat. Add chicken and brown on all sides, about 10 minutes. Transfer chicken to a heavy casserole or baking dish.

Place the frying pan back onto the burner on medium-high heat. Sauté onion, carrots, rutabaga, fennel, celery, potato and garlic until onions are soft, 5 to 10 minutes. Add tomato paste, white wine, rosemary, thyme, bay leaf and clove-studded onion. Stir together well and pour over chicken. Top up with stock. Drain pre-soaked white beans and add. Season with salt and pepper.

Cover tightly with a lid or aluminum foil and bake in the oven for 2 hours.

BREAD TOPPING While the dish is in the oven, make the bread topping. Mix together bread crumbs, parsley and melted butter (or olive oil) in a bowl.

Remove the cassoulet from the oven and uncover. Scatter the bread crumb mixture evenly on top. Return to the oven, uncovered, and bake until bread crumbs turn light brown, about 60 minutes.

To serve, ladle onto warmed plates or into large bowls.

WINE Red: Côtes de Ventoux · White: Côtes du Luberon

BREAD TOPPING

3	cups coarse fresh bread crumbs	750 mL
2 Tbsp.	chopped fresh parsley	30 mL
2 Tbsp.	butter, melted, or olive oil	30 mL

4 to 6 servings

Poached Halibut in Saffron-Tomato Broth with Ruby Chard

BROTH

2 Tbsp.	olive oil	30 mL
1	medium onion, sliced	1
1	fennel bulb, peeled and sliced	1
4	garlic cloves, sliced	4
¼ cup	dry sherry	60 mL
1	can Roma (plum) tomatoes (28 oz./ 796 mL)	1
3 cups	water	750 mL
	Pinch of saffron	
1 Tbsp.	sugar	15 mL

SEAFOOD AND CHARD

1 lb.	fresh clams, in the shell	500 g
1 lb.	fresh mussels, in the shell	500 g
4	skinless boneless halibut fillets (each 4 oz./125 g)	4
1	bunch ruby chard, stems removed	1

4 servings

This dish is a celebration of winter ingredients and simplicity. You will be able to taste all of the natural flavours of the delicately cooked seafood and braised chard.

TO MAKE BROTH Heat olive oil in a saucepan on medium-high heat. Sauté onion, fennel and garlic until softened, about 5 minutes.

Deglaze the pan by adding sherry and stirring to loosen the browned bits on the bottom. Add tomatoes, water, saffron and sugar. Simmer, uncovered, until well cooked, about 30 minutes. Strain the broth through a coarse sieve.

SEAFOOD AND CHARD Tap any clams and mussels whose shells are open; discard those that do not close.

Place halibut in a large saucepan and cover with broth. Put a lid on the pan and cook on medium heat until fish just starts to change colour, 5 to 10 minutes. Add clams and mussels, then cover with chard. Replace the lid on the pot and continue cooking until the shells open, about 5 minutes. Discard any clams or mussels whose shells have not opened.

To serve, remove chard from the saucepan and divide evenly among warmed soup bowls. Place halibut on top of chard and arrange clams and mussels around the sides. Ladle broth over top.

WINE Red: lightly chilled Pinot Noir · White: Viognier

Poached halibut in saffron-tomato broth with ruby chard >

Grilled Prawns with Pumpkin Risotto

4 cups	chicken, fish or vegetable stock	1 L
2 Tbsp.	butter	30 mL
1 cup	onion, ¼-inch/6-mm dice	250 mL
1 tsp.	minced garlic	5 mL
¼ cup	chopped fresh thyme	60 mL
2 cups	pumpkin, peeled, ½-inch/1-cm dice	500 mL
2 cups	arborio rice	500 mL
	Salt and freshly ground black pepper	
½ cup	dry white wine	125 mL
1 cup	whipping cream	250 mL
¼ cup	grated Parmesan cheese	60 mL
1 cup	chopped spinach leaves	250 mL

PRAWNS

2 Tbsp.	butter, melted	30 mL
1	garlic clove, minced	1
1 Tbsp.	chopped fresh parsley	15 mL
1½ lb.	prawn tails, peeled and deveined	750 g
	Sprigs of fresh thyme for garnish	

4 to 6 servings

On the west coast, we use spot prawns, a local variety that is very special to us because they are so tender and sweet. When simply grilled like this, they make a perfect accompaniment to the rich creamy risotto. Other prawns will also work well, of course.

TO MAKE RISOTTO Place stock in a saucepan and bring to a simmer on low heat. Keep hot.

Melt butter in a saucepan on medium heat. Sauté onion, garlic and thyme until softened, 2 to 3 minutes. Add pumpkin and rice, then sauté until rice grains are slightly transparent, 4 to 5 minutes. Season with salt and pepper.

Deglaze the pan by adding white wine and stirring to loosen the browned bits on the bottom. Add enough hot stock to cover rice by ½ inch/1 cm. Simmer, uncovered, on medium heat; stir constantly and add stock ½ cup/125 mL at a time as necessary to keep rice covered. After 20 minutes, start tasting the rice for doneness; it should be tender but not mushy (could take up to 30 minutes to cook).

When rice is 90 per cent cooked, stir in cream, Parmesan and spinach. Continue cooking until still creamy but thick enough to mound slightly on the plate, 3 to 4 minutes. Remove from the heat and keep warm.

PRAWNS Preheat the grill or barbecue on medium-high heat. Combine melted butter, garlic and parsley in a bowl.

Grill prawns, basting with butter mixture, until pink and cooked through, 1 to 2 minutes per side.

To serve, ladle 1 to 1½ cups/250 to 375 mL of risotto per serving onto warmed plates and arrange prawns on top. Garnish with a sprig of fresh thyme.

WINE Pinot Gris or Chardonnay

Steamed Smoked Black Cod with Herb-Horseradish Sabayon

Black cod, or sablefish has a tender, flaky, buttery texture. Unsmoked sablefish is sold in Asian markets, fresh or frozen. The smoked version is usually called smoked Alaskan black cod. We have found that simmering smoked black cod in lots of water with a small amount of pepper helps to remove any excess salt while preserving its light texture. Serve this dish with Truffled Brandade Cakes (page 133) and steamed greens, such as kale or chard.

TO MAKE REDUCTION Combine tarragon vinegar, shallots, garlic and pepper in a small saucepan on medium heat; simmer, uncovered, until reduced by half, about 5 minutes. Add white wine and thyme, and continue simmering, uncovered, until reduced by half, for another 5 minutes. Strain and cool.

FISH Place fish fillets in a large frying pan and season with pepper. Add enough cold water to cover fish, place a tight-fitting lid on the pan, and bring up to a simmer on high heat. Turn down the heat to medium-low and simmer for 8 minutes.

SABAYON While the fish is cooking, make the sabayon. Combine tarragon reduction, egg yolks and horseradish in a stainless steel bowl. Place the bowl over hot, but not simmering, water in a saucepan on medium heat; beat mixture until light, fluffy and hot to the touch, 4 to 5 minutes. Whisk in room-temperature butter 1 Tbsp/30 mL at a time until it is all incorporated. Season with salt. Stir in chopped chives and parsley.

To serve, remove fish fillets from the frying pan and blot with a paper towel to remove excess water. Place one fillet on each warmed plate and drizzle with sabayon.

WINE Red: Pinot Noir · White: Semillon

TARRAGON REDUCTION

½ cup	tarragon vinegar	125 mL
2	shallots, sliced	2
1	garlic clove, sliced	1
1 tsp.	cracked black pepper	5 mL
1 cup	dry white wine	250 mL
2	sprigs fresh thyme	2

FISH

4	smoked Alaskan black cod fillets (each 4 oz./125 g)	4
	Pinch of freshly ground black pepper	

SABAYON

1	recipe tarragon reduction	1
3	egg yolks	3
1 tsp.	grated fresh or prepared horseradish	5 mL
½ cup	butter, room temperature	125 g
	Salt	
2 Tbsp.	chopped fresh chives	30 mL
2 Tbsp.	chopped fresh parsley	30 mL

4 servings

New Potatoes with Lemon and Parsley

2 lb.	new potatoes	1 kg
2 Tbsp.	butter or olive oil	30 mL
2 Tbsp.	fresh lemon juice	30 mL
2 Tbsp.	chopped fresh parsley	30 mL
1 tsp.	sea salt	5 mL

4 servings

Imagine the first of the season's tiny new potatoes freshly dug from the earth, scrubbed and just steamed or boiled for a few minutes until fork tender. They make a fresh and simple accompaniment to almost any dish.

TO MAKE Place potatoes in a saucepan and cover with water. Bring to a boil on medium-high heat and cook until tender, about 10 to 15 minutes. Drain.

To serve, place potatoes in a bowl and tumble together with butter (or olive oil), lemon juice, parsley and sea salt.

Grilled Asparagus Spears with Raspberry-Shallot Vinaigrette

This simple dish is designed to accent the flavour of fresh asparagus, lightly grilled, either as a course on its own or as an accompaniment to a spring meal.

TO MAKE Fill a large bowl with ice-cold water and ice cubes. Bring a saucepan of salted water to a boil. Snap off and discard the woody bottoms of asparagus stalks. Place asparagus in boiling water for 1 minute, then plunge into the ice-cold water.

To make vinaigrette, heat 2 Tbsp./30 mL of the extra-virgin olive oil in a frying pan on medium heat. Sauté shallots until tender, 2 to 3 minutes. Remove from the stove and stir in raspberry vinegar and the remaining olive oil. Set aside.

Preheat the barbecue or a cast-iron grill pan on medium heat.

Drain asparagus and pat dry. Drizzle with a minimal amount of vegetable oil. Grill until lightly charred all over, about 4 to 5 minutes.

To serve, place asparagus in a bowl, add vinaigrette and toss gently. Season to taste with salt and pepper.

1 lb.	asparagus	500 g
½ cup	extra-virgin olive oil	125 mL
2	shallots, sliced thinly	2
¼ cup	raspberry vinegar	60 mL
	Vegetable oil	
	Salt and freshly ground black pepper	

4 servings

Balsamic and Honey Glazed Carrots

1 lb.	baby carrots, peeled	500 g
1 tsp.	butter	5 mL
1 cup	water	250 mL
¼ cup	honey	60 mL
¼ cup	balsamic vinegar	60 mL
	Salt and freshly ground black pepper	

4 servings

I love cooking with honey, and I try to use it in place of sugar whenever I can. Honey has a different kind of sweetness and also provides an added textural dimension, especially when used to glaze root vegetables like these carrots. The balsamic vinegar adds sweetness and a touch of acidity. These carrots are an excellent accompaniment to roasted meat or poultry.

TO MAKE Place carrots, butter and water in a shallow saucepan; bring to a boil on high heat. Reduce the heat to medium, cover and simmer until carrots are almost cooked, about 10 minutes.

Remove the lid, drain, and then stir in honey and balsamic vinegar. Increase heat to medium-high and simmer, uncovered, until liquid is mostly reduced and carrots are coated with a syrupy glaze, 5 to 7 minutes.

To serve, place glazed carrots in a warmed serving dish. Season to taste with salt and pepper.

Honey mustard free-range chicken breast (recipe page 74);
morel mushroom risotto cake (recipe page 118);
balsamic and honey glazed carrots >

Morel Mushroom Risotto Cake

3 cups	chicken stock	750 mL
2 Tbsp.	butter	30 mL
1 cup	thinly sliced morel mushrooms	250 mL
¼ cup	celery, ¼-inch/ 6-mm dice	60 mL
¼ cup	onion, ¼-inch/ 6-mm dice	60 mL
1 cup	arborio rice	250 mL
¼ cup	dry sherry	60 mL
	Salt and freshly ground black pepper	
1 Tbsp.	chopped fresh parsley	15 mL
1 Tbsp.	chopped fresh thyme	15 mL
	Rice flour for dredging	
¼ cup	vegetable oil	60 mL

4 large or 8 small cakes

These risotto cakes are an elegant alternative to potatoes to accompany fish, meat or chicken. I like them because they can be made a day ahead, so it's one less dish to prepare come dinnertime. Keep the risotto cakes refrigerated and well covered to prevent them from drying out. At the restaurant, we use metal ring molds to form the cakes, but at home I use a cut-down big yogurt container (for large cakes) or a round 3-inch/7.5-cm diameter cookie cutter (for small cakes).

The two-stage cooking method, as well as the dredging in rice flour before pan-frying, creates an excellent contrast in texture between the almost popcorn-like crispness of the outside and the creamy risotto of the centre.

In place of the mushrooms, try other ingredients such as sweet corn or sun-dried tomatoes.

TO MAKE Place stock in a saucepan and bring to a simmer on low heat. Keep hot.

Melt butter in another saucepan on medium heat. Sauté mushrooms, celery and onion until tender, but not brown, about 8 to 10 minutes. Add rice and stir until grains are coated with butter and slightly translucent, 2 to 3 minutes. Deglaze the pan by adding sherry and stirring to loosen the browned bits on the bottom.

Add enough hot stock to cover rice by ½ inch/1 cm. Simmer, uncovered, on medium heat; stir constantly and add stock ½ cup/125 mL at a time as necessary to keep rice covered. After 20 minutes, start tasting the rice for doneness; it should be tender but not mushy (could take up to 30 minutes to cook).

When rice is done, stir in parsley and thyme. While still warm, spoon risotto into 4 large or 8 small molds on a baking sheet lined with parchment paper. Cover and chill thoroughly in the refrigerator for at least 4 hours, preferably overnight. (Will keep refrigerated for 2 to 3 days.)

To serve, dredge risotto cakes in rice flour. Pan-fry two or three at a time in a small amount of the vegetable oil until golden brown on both sides and heated through, 3 to 4 minutes per side. Continue frying cakes, adding oil as needed, until all are done.

Lobster and Saffron Risotto

5 cups	shellfish stock (page 164)	1.25 L
½ cup	dry white wine	125 mL
	Pinch of saffron	
2 Tbsp.	butter	30 mL
1	small onion, ¼-inch/6-mm dice	1
1	large carrot, ¼-inch/6-mm dice	1
2	celery ribs, ¼-inch/6-mm dice	2
2	garlic cloves, minced	2
2	cups carnaroli or arborio rice	500 mL
¼ cup	grated Parmesan cheese	60 mL
¼ cup	whipping cream	60 mL
	Salt and freshly ground black pepper	
½ lb.	lobster meat, ½-inch/1-cm dice	250 g

4 to 6 servings

Lobster and saffron make perfect partners. Saffron is a very special spice that is expensive, but this recipe calls for only a small amount of it. We've found that pre-soaking the saffron threads in a liquid such as wine or stock brings out even more flavour and colour. For this risotto, we prefer to use carnaroli rice, which is a higher grade of Italian rice than arborio. Its grains are harder, allowing the risotto to keep a little more texture and definition when it is cooked.

For a variation, try using other types of seafood, such as fresh shrimp or crab.

TO MAKE Place stock in a large saucepan and bring to a simmer on low heat. Keep hot.

Place white wine and saffron threads in a bowl.

Melt butter in a saucepan on medium heat. Sauté onion, carrot, celery and garlic until tender, 8 to 10 minutes. Add rice and sauté until grains are covered with butter and are slightly translucent, 2 to 3 minutes.

Deglaze the pan by adding white wine mixture and stirring to loosen the browned bits on the bottom. Add enough hot stock to cover rice by ½ inch/1 cm. Simmer, uncovered, on medium heat; stir constantly and add stock ½ cup/125 mL at a time as necessary to keep rice covered. After 20 minutes, start tasting the rice for doneness; it should be tender but not mushy (could take as long as 30 minutes to cook).

When rice is done, stir in Parmesan cheese and whipping cream. Season with salt and pepper to taste. Fold in lobster meat and serve.

Roasted Sweet Bell Peppers with Balsamic Vinaigrette

These oven-roasted sweet bell peppers make a good addition to any meal. You can make them ahead and store them in the refrigerator for a few days. Just make sure you take them out prior to serving, so that they are not too cold when you eat them. As an extra touch, I like to garnish this dish with a twist or two of freshly ground black pepper and a scattering of chopped fresh basil leaves.

6	bell peppers, assorted colours	6
	Vegetable oil	
2 Tbsp.	balsamic vinegar	30 mL
¼ cup	olive oil	60 mL

4 servings

TO MAKE Preheat the oven to 400°F/200°C.

Rub peppers with small amount of vegetable oil. Place in a shallow pan and roast until skins blister and are lightly coloured, 15 to 20 minutes.

Place peppers in a bowl, cover tightly with plastic wrap and let sit for 20 minutes to loosen skins. Peel peppers and remove seeds. Tear peeled peppers into strips.

To serve, place pepper strips in a bowl; toss with balsamic vinegar and olive oil.

Roasted Yam and Sweet Potato Phyllo Rolls

These yam and sweet potatoes in phyllo are very popular at our house. Slicing them in half diagonally makes for a more elegant presentation. You can use a variety of different fillings, such as artichoke hearts with Parmesan cheese and prosciutto, or Chinese cabbage with shiitake mushrooms.

TO MAKE Preheat the oven to 400°F/200°C and line a baking sheet with parchment paper.

Melt butter in a frying pan on medium heat and sauté onion until softened, 2 to 3 minutes. Add yam and sweet potatoes and toss until well coated with butter. Add thyme and season to taste with sea salt and pepper.

Transfer to an ovenproof dish and roast, uncovered, until tender, about 30 minutes, stirring occasionally. Remove from the oven and cool. Refrigerate for 1 hour.

Fold each sheet of phyllo pastry in half to make a rectangle approximately 8 by 12 inches/20 by 30 cm. Place the pastry sheets on a cutting board with the short side facing you. Brush with some of the melted butter. Place a quarter of the filling along the bottom edge of each pastry rectangle, leaving 1 inch/2.5 cm along the sides uncovered by the filling. Fold the sides of the pastry over the filling, then fold up the pastry from the bottom to cover the filling and roll up into a loose cylinder about 1 inch/2.5 cm in diameter and 6 inches/15 cm long.

Place pastries seam-side down on the prepared baking sheet and brush tops with the remaining melted butter.

Bake until pastry is golden and crisp, and filling is heated through, about 15 minutes. Serve immediately.

2 Tbsp.	butter	30 mL
1	small onion, ½-inch/1-cm dice	1
8 oz.	yam, peeled ½-inch/1-cm dice	250 g
8 oz.	sweet potatoes, peeled, ½-inch/1-cm dice	250 g
1 tsp.	chopped fresh thyme leaves	5 mL
	Sea salt and pepper	
4	sheets frozen phyllo pastry, thawed	4
2 Tbsp.	butter, melted	30 mL

4 servings

< Roast pork tenderloin with savoury sausage stuffing
(recipe page 80); roasted yam and sweet potato phyllo rolls

Summer Vegetable Succotash

2 Tbsp.	olive oil	30 mL
½ cup	onion, ¼-inch/ 6-mm dice	125 mL
1	garlic clove, minced	1
1 cup	zucchini, ¼-inch/ 6-mm dice	250 mL
1 cup	red pepper, ¼-inch/ 6-mm dice	250 mL
½ cup	tomato, ¼-inch/ 6-mm dice	125 mL
1 cup	fresh corn kernels	250 mL
2 Tbsp.	chopped fresh parsley	30 mL
2 Tbsp.	chopped fresh basil	30 mL
	Salt and freshly ground black pepper	

4 servings

This is our northern version of the classic southern comfort food called succotash. It's a midsummer celebration of the first picked sweet corn and is a colourful accompaniment to either chicken or grilled seafood.

Our favourite kind of corn to use is Peaches & Cream, for its sweet flavour and pretty mixture of white and yellow kernels. Instead of zucchini, you can use any other type of summer squash.

TO MAKE Heat olive oil in a frying pan on medium heat. Sauté onion and garlic until translucent, 2 to 3 minutes. Add zucchini and red pepper; sauté until slightly softened, 5 to 6 minutes. Add tomato and corn, then simmer, uncovered, just until vegetables are cooked through, about 10 minutes. Stir in parsley and basil, then season with salt and pepper. Serve at once.

Chanterelle and Sweet Corn Risotto

Risotto is a dish that will take your full attention to prepare. You'll just have to stay in the kitchen while you make it, so pour yourself a glass of wine, relax and get ready to stir, stir, stir. The secret to making risotto is to add the liquid gradually and to stir frequently. Think of it as therapy. This vegetarian risotto can also be served as an appetizer.

TO MAKE If mushrooms are small, leave whole. Halve or slice large mushrooms.

Place corn broth (or stock) in a saucepan and bring to a simmer on low heat. Keep hot.

Melt butter in a saucepan on medium heat. Sauté onion, garlic and sage until onion is almost translucent, about 5 minutes. Add mushrooms and sauté until lightly coloured, 2 to 3 minutes. Add rice and sauté until grains are covered with butter and are slightly translucent, 2 to 3 minutes. Season with salt and pepper.

Deglaze the pan by adding white wine and stirring to loosen the browned bits on the bottom. Stir in corn. Add enough stock to cover rice by ½ inch/1 cm. Simmer, uncovered, on medium heat; stir constantly and add stock ½ cup/125 mL at a time as necessary to keep rice covered. After 20 minutes, start tasting the rice for doneness; it should be tender but not mushy (could take up to 30 minutes to cook).

When rice is done, stir in whipping cream, Parmesan cheese and spinach. Cook until mixture is still creamy but thick enough to mound slightly on a plate, about 2 to 3 minutes. Serve hot.

2 cups	chanterelle mushrooms	500 mL
4 cups	sweet corn broth (page 165) or chicken stock	1 L
2 Tbsp.	butter	30 mL
1 cup	onion, ¼-inch/ 6-mm dice	250 mL
1 tsp.	minced garlic	5 mL
¼ cup	chopped fresh sage	60 mL
2 cups	carnaroli or arborio rice	500 mL
	Salt and freshly ground black pepper	
½ cup	dry white wine	125 mL
1 cup	fresh corn kernels	250 mL
½ cup	whipping cream	125 mL
¼ cup	grated Parmesan cheese	60 mL
1 cup	coarsely chopped spinach leaves	250 mL

4 to 6 servings

Sweet Potato and Celery Root Purée

1 lb.	sweet potatoes	500 g
1 lb.	celery root	500 g
½ cup	whipping cream, warmed	125 mL
2 Tbsp.	butter	30 mL
	Salt and freshly ground black pepper	

4 servings

This combination of puréed sweet potato and celery root goes well with either turkey or chicken. I like cooking with celery root, because it has great flavour, and texturally it is very interesting. Fortunately, it is now becoming more available in markets. Buy the larger ones if you can, because you lose a lot when trimming and peeling, especially the top of the celery root, which can be sandy even after a good washing.

TO MAKE Peel sweet potatoes and celery root and cut into roughly 2-inch/5-cm cubes. Place in a saucepan with enough water to cover and bring to a boil on medium-high heat. Turn down the heat to medium and simmer, uncovered, until tender, 15 to 20 minutes.

Remove from the stove and drain well. Place in a blender or food processor. Add warmed whipping cream and butter, then purée. Season to taste with salt and pepper. Serve hot.

Fall Vegetable Gratin

This is a tasty side dish when you want something you can prepare ahead and stick in the oven an hour before dinner. Feel free to use different vegetables that you may have on hand for this, as long as they don't get too watery when cooked. Fennel bulb, turnip, leek, sweet potato and broccoli are all excellent additions.

TO MAKE Preheat the oven to 375°F/190°C and butter a small casserole dish.

Bring a saucepan of salted water to a boil. Mix together carrot, parsnip, celery root and cauliflower in a bowl, then blanch lightly in the boiling water to soften slightly, 2 to 3 minutes. Drain well.

Place vegetable mixture in the prepared casserole dish. Season with salt and pepper. Whisk together whipping cream and eggs in a bowl; pour over vegetables and pack them down lightly.

Combine bread crumbs, Parmesan cheese and parsley in a bowl, then sprinkle evenly over vegetables. (At this point, you can refrigerate the dish for finishing later.)

Bake in the oven until golden brown on top, about 40 minutes. Remove from the oven and serve hot.

1	large carrot, peeled and grated	1
1	large parsnip, peeled and grated	1
1	celery root, peeled and grated	1
1 cup	finely chopped cauliflower	250 mL
	Salt and freshly ground black pepper	
1 cup	whipping cream	250 mL
2	eggs	2
1 cup	coarse fresh bread crumbs	250 mL
¼ cup	grated Parmesan cheese	60 mL
2 Tbsp.	chopped fresh parsley	30 mL

4 to 6 servings

Roasted Butternut Squash
with Maple-Thyme Butter

1 lb.	butternut squash	500 g
2 Tbsp.	butter, melted	30 mL
2 Tbsp.	maple syrup	30 mL
1 Tbsp.	chopped fresh thyme	15 mL
½ cup	chicken stock	125 mL
	Salt	

4 servings

This roasted squash is one of my favourite vegetable dishes. It tastes wonderfully sweet, and the texture is smooth and creamy when baked like this.

TO MAKE Preheat the oven to 400°F/200°C.

Peel squash and cut in half lengthwise. Scoop out and discard seeds, then cut into slices ½ inch/1 cm thick. Place in an ovenproof dish.

Mix together melted butter, maple syrup, thyme and stock in a bowl; pour over squash. Bring to a simmer on medium-high heat. Put a lid on the dish and bake in the oven until squash is tender, 15 to 20 minutes. Season to taste with salt. Serve hot.

Grilled beef tenderloin with olive oil-poached Yukon Gold potatoes and blue cheese (recipe page 92); roasted butternut squash with maple-thyme butter >

Sunday Vegetable Hash

3	medium potatoes	3
1	medium onion	1
2	celery ribs	2
2	medium carrots	2
½	fennel bulb (optional)	½
¼ cup	vegetable oil	60 mL
1 tsp.	chopped fresh thyme leaves	
	Sea salt and freshly ground black pepper	
1 Tbsp.	chopped fresh parsley	15 mL

4 to 6 servings

This recipe is my answer to the often-asked question, "What can I make for lunch?" Most people nearly always have the basic mix of carrots, onions and celery in the refrigerator. To these, simply add whatever else you have in the way of vegetables, such as yams, sweet potatoes or sweet bell peppers. This hash makes an excellent side dish for a brunch and is also very good with poultry.

If you want a heartier dish for a light lunch, cook the hash, then top it with thick slices of aged cheddar cheese and broil until the cheese is melted and golden in colour, about 5 to 6 minutes.

TO MAKE Preheat the oven to 375°F/190°C.

Peel and cut potatoes, onion, celery, carrots and fennel (optional) into roughly 1-inch/2.5-cm dice. Pat potato cubes dry with a paper towel.

Heat vegetable oil in a large frying pan on medium-high heat. Sauté potatoes until they start to brown, about 10 minutes. Add onion, celery, carrots and fennel (optional); sauté for a further 5 minutes. Add thyme. Season to taste with sea salt and pepper.

Transfer to a roasting pan and bake until done, about 20 minutes. Garnish with chopped parsley and serve hot.

Potato, Herb and Onion Latkes

When it comes to potato latkes, everyone seems to have a special way of making them. This recipe has been well tested over time at Bishop's Restaurant, and we often get requests for them. Most of the time, we serve the latkes with salmon, but they can be served with almost anything, or even by themselves as a light lunch with a dollop of sour cream.

TO MAKE Peel and quarter potatoes. Place potatoes, onion, egg, mustard, parsley, lemon juice and salt in a food processor and purée. Add flour and mix well.

Heat a small amount of the vegetable oil in a large heavy frying pan. Ladle ¼ cup/60 mL batter for each latke and fry 2 or 3 at a time until golden brown on both sides, about 3 to 4 minutes per side. Use up the remaining batter, adding oil as necessary. Makes about 12 latkes, 3 inches/ 7.5 cm in diameter.

Blot latkes on paper towels and serve hot.

1 lb.	russet or Yukon Gold potatoes	500 g
½ cup	onion, 1-inch/ 2.5-cm dice	125 mL
1	egg	1
1 Tbsp.	grainy mustard	15 mL
2 Tbsp.	chopped fresh parsley	30 mL
1	lemon, juiced	1
1 tsp.	salt	5 mL
⅔ cup	flour	150 mL
¼ cup	vegetable oil	60 mL

4 to 6 servings

Truffles are perhaps the world's most elusive and expensive fungi, but don't despair, because you can get the flavour you need for this dish by using a good truffle-flavoured olive oil.

Brandade is a traditional dish from the south of France, made by cooking salt cod, potatoes and truffles, then mashing them with olive oil. We developed this variation on that recipe as an accompaniment to the Steamed Smoked Black Cod with Herb-Horseradish Sabayon (page 111).

Russet potatoes are also called Idaho or baking potatoes.

TO MAKE Place whole potatoes into a soup pot, cover with cold water and bring to a boil on medium-high heat. (Do not add salt to the water, as it causes the exterior of the potatoes to flake.) Simmer, uncovered, until partially cooked, about 15 minutes. Drain well and cool for 20 minutes.

Place smoked cod (or smoked salmon) in a saucepan and cover with water. Bring to a boil on medium-high heat and simmer until well cooked, 8 to 10 minutes. Drain and flake.

Grate cooked potatoes and mix well with smoked fish, truffle oil, green onions and parsley in a bowl. Season with salt and pepper. Shape into a log 4 inches/10 cm in diameter. Wrap in plastic wrap and chill thoroughly in the refrigerator for at least 4 hours, preferably overnight. (Will keep in the refrigerator for 2 to 3 days.)

To serve, cut into slices ½ inch/1 cm thick. Heat a little of the vegetable oil in a large frying pan on medium heat and pan-fry 1 or 2 slices at a time until golden and crispy and cooked through, 4 to 5 minutes per side. Fry the remaining slices, adding oil as necessary. Serve hot.

2 lb.	russet, Kennebec or other starchy potato, peeled	1 kg
4 oz.	smoked black cod or smoked salmon	125 g
1 Tbsp.	truffle oil	15 mL
1	bunch green onions, finely chopped	1
2 Tbsp.	chopped fresh parsley	30 mL
	Salt and freshly ground black pepper	
¼ cup	vegetable oil	60 mL

4 to 6 servings

< Steamed smoked black cod with herb-horseradish
  sabayon (recipe page 111); truffled brandade cakes

Yam, Potato and Celery Hash

1	large yam	1
1	large potato	1
1	small onion	1
3	celery ribs	3
½ cup	olive oil	125 mL
2	garlic cloves, chopped	2
1	sprig fresh thyme	1
	Salt and freshly ground black pepper	

4 servings

These oven-roasted winter vegetables are good served alongside roasted poultry such as duck or chicken. They also make a hearty brunch when served with crispy fried bacon and poached eggs.

TO MAKE Preheat the oven to 375°F/190°C.

Peel and cut yam, potato and onion into roughly 1-inch/ 2.5-cm dice. Cut celery into 1-inch/2.5-cm dice.

Pour olive oil into a shallow roasting pan, then place the pan in the oven to heat for 5 to 10 minutes.

Remove the pan from the oven and add vegetable mixture and chopped garlic, tossing to coat vegetables evenly with hot oil. Add thyme, leaving it whole so that it will be easy to remove later. Season to taste with salt and pepper.

Place vegetables back in the oven and roast, uncovered, until tender, about 45 minutes. Stir occasionally, being careful not to mash vegetables. Remove and discard thyme. Serve hot.

Oven-braised Celery

Braised celery makes a fine accompaniment to any roasted meat or poultry, and it is very easy to prepare. Just make sure that you discard any of the tough outer stalks and wash the celery really well before cooking.

TO MAKE Preheat the oven to 400°F/200°C.

Cut each celery bunch lengthwise into quarters, leaving each quarter still attached at the stem end.

Melt butter in a frying pan on medium heat and sauté celery lightly, about 5 minutes. Transfer to an oven-proof dish. Season with salt and pepper, then add thyme and stock. Cover and bake in the oven until tender, 15 to 20 minutes. Serve hot.

2	bunches celery	2
2 Tbsp.	butter	30 mL
	Salt and freshly ground black pepper	
1 tsp.	chopped fresh thyme	5 mL
1 cup	chicken stock	250 mL

4 servings

DESSERTS

Almond Tuiles with Rhubarb Mousse

½ cup	sugar	125 mL
½ cup	flour	125 mL
¼ tsp.	salt	1 mL
¼ cup	ground almonds	60 mL
½ tsp.	ground cinnamon	2.5 mL
4	egg whites	4
3 Tbsp.	butter, melted	45 mL

Tuile is the French word for "tulip," and that is the shape you want when forming these delicate cookie cups to hold the rhubarb mousse. You can also fill these cups with fresh berries or ice cream.

TO MAKE TUILES Place sugar, flour, salt, ground almonds and cinnamon in an electric mixer; beat until well combined. Add egg whites and melted butter; mix well. Allow dough to rest for 1 hour before using.

Preheat the oven to 325°F/160°C and line a baking sheet with parchment paper.

Use a small offset spatula to spread dough very thinly on the prepared baking sheet, to form rounds 5 inches/ 13 cm in diameter. Bake in the oven until golden, 5 to 7 minutes. Makes about 8 tuiles.

Remove from the oven and, while the tuiles are warm, press them into muffin tins or small ramekins and shape to form cups. Allow to cool, then store in a tightly covered container until needed. (Tuiles can be made ahead and will keep for up to a week.)

MOUSSE Place rhubarb, water and ½ cup/125 mL of the sugar in a small saucepan that has a tight-fitting lid. Bring to a simmer, uncovered, on medium heat. Cover, turn down the heat to low and cook until rhubarb is soft, about 20 minutes. Remove from the stove and allow to cool for 15 minutes.

Transfer to a blender or food processor and purée. Place 1 cup/250 mL of rhubarb purée in a small saucepan and sprinkle with gelatin. (Any remaining purée can be frozen for later use in more tuiles or as a dessert sauce.)

Once gelatin begins to dissolve, cook purée on medium-low heat, stirring gently, until gelatin is fully dissolved. Stir in the remaining sugar and Grand Marnier (or other orange liqueur), then remove from the stove. Allow to cool to room temperature.

In a bowl, mix cream with vanilla extract, then whip until stiff. Fold rhubarb mixture into whipped cream. Cover and chill in the refrigerator.

To serve, fill one tuile per person with mousse and place on a dessert plate. Garnish with mint leaves.

MOUSSE

1 lb.	rhubarb, sliced	500 g
½ cup	water	125 mL
1 cup	sugar	250 mL
1	envelope gelatin	1
2 oz.	Grand Marnier or other orange liqueur	60 mL
1 cup	whipping cream	250 mL
½ tsp.	vanilla extract	2.5 mL
	Fresh mint leaves for garnish	

8 servings

Meyer Lemon Brûlée Tart with Lavender Pastry

PASTRY

¾ cup	flour	175 mL
1 tsp.	chopped lavender	5 mL
½ tsp.	sugar	2.5 mL
½ tsp.	salt	2.5 mL
6 Tbsp.	butter, softened	90 mL
1 Tbsp.	cold water	15 mL

Meyer lemons appear in our local markets for just the briefest of moments in the early spring, and to quote Bishop's Restaurant senior sous-chef Jeff, "Their complex floral aromas and flavours make them a joy to cook with." They are juicy and have a hint of a grapefruit aftertaste, making them a favourite for citrus desserts. If you cannot find Meyer lemons, you can use regular lemons.

TO MAKE PASTRY Combine flour, lavender, sugar and salt in a bowl. Add softened butter and mix until the texture becomes coarse and mealy. Add water and combine well, taking care not to overmix the dough.

Flatten dough into a disk and wrap in plastic wrap. Allow to rest for 30 minutes before using. (Forming dough into a disk rather than a ball will make it easier to roll out into a round later, especially if you are making the dough ahead of time and will be refrigerating it.)

Preheat the oven to 350°F/175°C.

On a lightly floured surface, roll out pastry to form a round 12 inches/30 cm in diameter. Line a 10-inch/25-cm tart pan with the pastry round, and use the back of the tines of a fork to press down around the edge. Line the bottom of the tart with a piece of parchment paper and fill with dried beans. (The dried beans, which keep the bottom of the tart shell flat while baking, can be kept and reused for this purpose.) Bake for 20 minutes, until pastry just begins to colour around the edges and bottom looks set. Remove the beans and allow pie shell to cool while you make the filling. Turn down the oven temperature to 300°F/150°C.

FILLING Whisk together eggs and sugar in a bowl until smooth and sugar is dissolved. Stir in lemon zest and juice, then whisk in whipping cream.

Pour filling into tart shell and bake until set, about 30 minutes. Check for doneness by tapping the edge of the pan; the centre of the tart should barely wiggle. Allow to cool to room temperature, then refrigerate to chill thoroughly.

Sprinkle sugar for caramelizing evenly on top of tart. Use a small propane or butane torch to heat the sugar until it melts and is golden. Cut the tart into slices immediately, before the caramelized sugar hardens, and serve.

FILLING

5	eggs	5
2 cups	sugar	500 mL
4	Meyer (or other) lemons, zest and juice	4
1 cup	whipping cream	250 mL
½ cup	sugar for caramelizing	125 mL

Yields 1 tart, 10 inches/25 cm in diameter

Rhubarb Upside-down Cake

1 lb.	rhubarb	500 g
¼ cup	butter, melted	60 mL
⅔ cup	brown sugar	150 mL
1½ cups	flour	375 mL
1 tsp.	baking powder	5 mL
½ tsp.	baking soda	2.5 mL
½ tsp.	salt	2.5 mL
½ cup	butter, softened	125 mL
½ cup	sugar	125 mL
2	eggs	2
½ cup	milk	125 mL
1	orange, zest and juice	1
	Vanilla ice cream or whipped cream	

Yields 6 ramekins, each 8 oz./250 mL,
or 1 cake, 8 inches/20 cm square

These individual cakes are a breeze to make, and they go into the oven just after the appetizer has gone out to the table. I like the contrast between hot and cold, when the cakes are served warm topped with vanilla ice cream. For a special garnish, sprinkle with chopped candied ginger.

TO MAKE Preheat the oven to 350°F/175°C.

Cut rhubarb stalks in half horizontally along their length, then slice into pieces 1 inch/2.5 cm thick.

Brush the insides of ramekins (or cake pan) with melted butter and sprinkle with brown sugar. Cover the bottom of each ramekin (or cake pan) with sliced rhubarb.

Sift together flour, baking powder, baking soda and salt into a bowl.

Place softened butter and sugar in an electric mixer; beat until light and fluffy. Add eggs and mix until well combined. Add milk, orange zest and juice, and flour mixture. Mix well.

Fill each ramekin two thirds full with batter (or pour all the batter into the cake pan). Bake ramekins in the oven for 25 to 30 minutes (bake cake pan for 45 to 50 minutes). Check for doneness by inserting a toothpick into the centre; it should come out clean when done. Remove from the oven and allow to cool for 10 minutes.

To serve ramekins, invert cakes onto warmed dessert plates and top with either a scoop of vanilla ice cream (or a dollop of whipped cream). To serve whole cake, cut into squares and top with ice cream (or whipped cream)

Rhubarb upside-down cake >

Lemon-Orange Pound Cake
with Grand Marnier Glaze

CAKE

	Butter for greasing	
	Flour for dusting	
1 cup	butter	250 mL
2 cups	sugar	500 mL
4	eggs	4
3 cups	flour	750 mL
1 tsp.	baking powder	5 mL
1 cup	milk	250 mL
2	oranges, zest and juice	2
2	lemons, zest and juice	2

GLAZE

1	orange, zest and juice	1
1	lemon, zest and juice	1
1¼ cups	sugar	300 mL
2 oz.	Grand Marnier or other orange liqueur	60 mL

Yields 1 cake, 10 inches/25 cm in diameter

This moist and zesty glazed citrus pound cake is a classic—and what would we chefs do if we didn't have lemons and oranges to cook with? They play such a large part in any sweet or savoury culinary repertory. These days, citrus fruits are available all year round, but spring is actually their peak season.

TO MAKE CAKE Preheat the oven to 350°F/175°C. Grease and flour a deep 10-inch/25-cm cake (or springform) pan.

Cream butter and sugar together in an electric mixer, about 5 minutes. Add eggs one at a time, mixing in well.

Sift together flour and baking powder into a bowl. Alternately add half the flour mixture, then half the milk to the butter mixture, until all incorporated. Add zest and juice of oranges and lemons.

Pour batter into the prepared pan and bake until done, 45 to 55 minutes. Check for doneness by inserting a toothpick into the centre; it should come out clean when done.

GLAZE Strain lemon and orange juice. Place strained juice, zest, Grand Marnier (or other orange liqueur) and sugar in a saucepan; bring to a boil on high heat. Remove from the stove and cool to room temperature.

Brush the glaze over the cake while still warm, coating it well. Reserve any extra for drizzling later.

To serve, cut cake into pieces and drizzle with any remaining glaze.

Warm Blueberry Cake

This recipe comes from Dennis's Grandma Green, who makes this fabulous coffee cake with the fresh blueberries that grow in abundance on their lakefront property on Vancouver Island. The first time I áte it, I was amazed at how moist it was—and even more at how moist it still was the next day. This cake is best served slightly warm, with fresh whipped cream to accompany it.

You can also make this cake, like Mrs. Green, with fresh rhubarb in the spring. And at different times, depending on the season, I have made it with blackberries, cranberries and raspberries, always with excellent results.

TO MAKE Preheat the oven to 350°F/175°C and grease a 13 × 9-inch/33 × 23-cm cake pan; or 12 ramekins, each 4 oz./125 mL; or a cupcake pan.

Cream together butter and brown sugar in an electric mixer until light and fluffy, about 5 minutes. Add eggs and beat thoroughly.

Sift together flour, salt, baking soda, cinnamon and nutmeg into a bowl. Add half of the flour mixture and half of the buttermilk to the butter mixture in the mixer. Beat lightly. Add the remaining flour mixture and remaining buttermilk; mix until just combined. Remove the bowl from the mixer and fold in blueberries. Spoon batter into the prepared pan (or ramekins or cupcake pan).

Combine sugar, cinnamon and chopped pecans in a bowl. Sprinkle over top of batter.

Bake in the oven until done: 30 to 35 minutes for ramekins or cupcakes, 45 to 50 minutes for a large cake. Test for doneness by inserting a toothpick into the centre (or centres); it should come out clean when done. Remove from the oven and cool to room temperature. Serve while still slightly warm.

	Butter for greasing	
½ cup	butter	125 mL
1 cup	brown sugar	250 mL
2	eggs	2
2 cups	flour	500 mL
½ tsp.	salt	2.5 mL
1 tsp.	baking soda	5 mL
½ tsp.	ground cinnamon	2.5 mL
	Pinch of ground nutmeg	
¾ cup	buttermilk	175 mL
2 cups	fresh blueberries	500 mL
½ cup	sugar	125 mL
2 tsp.	cinnamon	10 mL
1 cup	chopped pecans	250 mL

Yields 1 cake, 13 × 9 inches/33 × 23 cm; or 12 ramekins or cupcakes, each 4 oz./125 mL

Gooseberry and Almond Crumble

	Butter for greasing	
¼ cup	brown sugar	60 mL
¼ cup	butter	60 mL
¼ cup	sliced almonds	60 mL
¼ cup	flour	60 mL
½ cup	rolled oats	125 mL
1 lb.	gooseberries, halved	500 g
¼ cup	sugar	60 mL
2 Tbsp.	flour	30 mL

Yields 1 pan, 8 inches/20 cm square

Gooseberries, with their tart flavour, have always been a favourite fruit for crumbles, as they get nice and soft under the crisp crust of brown sugar and oats (and in this case, almonds). At the restaurant, we prefer to use the natural sliced almonds, which have a better flavour than the blanched ones. For a variation, use blueberries, pitted cherries with a bit of ginger or pitted apricot halves. As these fruits are sweeter than gooseberries, you can use less sugar.

TO MAKE Preheat the oven to 375°F/190°C and grease an 8-inch/20-cm square ovenproof dish.

To make the topping, combine brown sugar, butter, sliced almonds, ¼ cup/60 mL flour and rolled oats in a bowl. Mix together well.

In another bowl, toss gooseberries with sugar and 2 Tbsp./30 mL flour, then place in the prepared ovenproof dish. Cover evenly with the topping.

Bake until the topping is golden brown and fruit is soft, about 45 minutes. Serve while still warm.

Poached Peaches in Raspberry Tisane Syrup

Herb teas, or tisanes, are a wonderful ingredient to use in recipes. We've found them to be very tasty as a poaching liquid for fresh fruit, as the base for a sorbet or even as the liquid in a rice dish. Here, the flavour of the raspberry with peaches (or apricots) is a wonderful complement, and tastes perfect served over a scoop of vanilla ice cream on a hot day.

2 cups	water	500 mL
1 cup	sugar	250 mL
2 bags	raspberry tea (or 1 Tbsp./ 15 mL loose)	2 bags
1 lb.	peaches or apricots	500 g

6 servings

TO MAKE Combine water and sugar in a saucepan and bring to a boil on high heat. Add tea and remove from the stove. Cover and allow to steep for 30 minutes, then strain tisane and set aside.

Fill a bowl with ice-cold water. Bring a medium pot of water to a boil. Score peaches with a paring knife and place them in the boiling water for 30 seconds, then plunge them into the ice-cold water.

Using a paring knife, remove and discard the skin from peaches. Run a knife down through the seam of the peach until you hit the stone. Turn the knife to remove the stone and cut peach in half.

(If you are using apricots, you do not need to blanch or peel them. Just cut them in half and remove the pits.)

Pour tisane into a saucepan and bring to a boil on medium heat. Add peaches (or apricots). Turn down the heat to medium-low and simmer, uncovered, until fruit is tender, about 15 minutes. Remove from the stove, allow fruit to cool in syrup, then refrigerate in a covered container. (Will keep in the refrigerator for up to a week.)

Serve fruit chilled, either on its own or with a little of the poaching syrup.

Summer Berry Parfait with Muscat Sabayon

Few fruits are as luscious and juicy as fresh berries at their peak in the summer. The parade of berries begins in early June with the first strawberries, followed throughout the course of the summer by raspberries, blueberries and blackberries.

A warm sabayon is the perfect way to top off a bowl of berries on top of ice cream. As you work your way through the layers, you will be treated to a mouthful of differing tastes, textures and temperatures, with the flavour of the berries shining through.

TO MAKE BERRIES Toss berries gently with icing sugar, pepper and mint in a bowl. Allow to marinate for 30 minutes.

SABAYON Combine egg yolk, icing sugar, muscat wine, orange zest and juice in a large stainless steel bowl. Place the bowl over a saucepan of simmering but not boiling water on medium heat, and whisk until sabayon is thickened and pale and hot to the touch.

To serve, place a scoop of vanilla ice cream in each bowl or parfait glass. Spoon berries over ice cream, then top with warm sabayon.

BERRIES

1 lb.	berries	500 g
2 Tbsp.	icing sugar	30 mL
	Pinch of freshly ground black pepper	
1 Tbsp.	finely chopped fresh mint leaves	15 mL

SABAYON

1	egg yolk	1
2 Tbsp.	icing sugar	30 mL
2 Tbsp.	muscat wine	30 mL
½ tsp.	orange zest	2.5 mL
2 Tbsp.	fresh orange juice	30 mL
	Vanilla ice cream	

4 servings

< Summer berry parfait with muscat sabayon

Spiced Poached Pears with Red Wine Caramel

PEARS

2 cups	dry red wine	500 mL
1 cup	water	250 mL
1 cup	sugar	250 mL
1	cinnamon stick	1
4	sprigs fresh basil	4
1	vanilla bean	1
6	large pears, peeled and cored	6

CARAMEL

1 cup	dry red wine	250 mL
1 cup	poaching liquid from pears	250 mL
2 Tbsp.	water	30 mL
½ cup	sugar	125 mL
	Blue cheese for garnish, optional	

Yields 6 servings

A beautiful whole poached pear sitting on a splash of red wine caramel, perhaps with a sliver of blue cheese alongside, makes the perfect light seasonal finish to an autumn meal. These poached pears will keep in their poaching liquid for up to a week, so you can make them when you have some time and refrigerate until needed. It is actually good to poach the pears at least a day ahead, as they will absorb the colour of the poaching liquid and turn a deep maroon colour. Choose pears that have the best shape and no blemishes for this dish.

TO POACH PEARS Place red wine, water, sugar, cinnamon stick and basil in a saucepan. Slice vanilla bean in half lengthwise, scrape out seeds, then add seeds and husk to wine mixture. Bring to a simmer on medium heat. Add pears and place a plate on top of them, to hold them under the liquid. Continue simmering until pears are tender, about 20 minutes.

Remove the saucepan from the stove and allow pears to cool in poaching liquid. Cover and refrigerate until needed. When you are ready to serve, remove pears from liquid and strain, reserving poaching liquid. Discard spices.

CARAMEL Heat red wine and poaching liquid in a saucepan on medium heat until simmering.

In a separate, heavy-bottomed saucepan, combine water and sugar. Boil on high heat, uncovered, until the golden caramel stage is reached, 5 to 10 minutes. Add wine mixture and continue boiling, uncovered, until caramel is reduced to 1 cup/250 mL, about 10 minutes. Strain.

To serve, drizzle each warmed plate with reduced caramel, and top with a poached pear. Garnish with a small piece of blue cheese (optional).

Fuji Apple Galette

Large Fuji apples, the size of a softball at times, are one of the best varieties for tarts and pies when you want the apple to retain some texture after baking. Other good varieties of apple for this include Gala and Spartan, but basically any type of fresh fruit or berry that you would put in a pie can be used to fill this galette.

A galette is perhaps the simplest of all fruit tarts, as it is made by forming a pastry round and folding it over a fruit filling, leaving a small hole in the centre at the top.

TO MAKE PASTRY Combine flour, sugar and salt in a bowl. Add softened butter and mix until the texture becomes coarse and mealy. Add water and combine well. Knead lightly until the dough forms a ball, taking care not to overmix. Wrap pastry in plastic wrap and allow to rest for 30 minutes before using.

Divide pastry into 6 portions. Roll out each portion on a lightly floured surface to form a round 6 inches/15 cm in diameter. Set aside.

GALETTES Preheat the oven to 375°F/190°C and line a baking sheet with parchment paper.

Combine sugar, cinnamon, cardamom, cloves and nutmeg in a bowl.

Place a small dab of butter and a sprinkle of spiced sugar mixture on each pastry round. Top each with slices from half an apple, another dab of butter and another sprinkle of spiced sugar. Fold up the pastry edges to encase the filling, leaving a small hole open in the centre.

Transfer galettes to the prepared baking sheet and bake until pastry is golden and apples are cooked, about 30 minutes. Allow to cool slightly. Serve on individual plates while still warm.

PASTRY		
1½ cups	flour	375 mL
1 tsp.	sugar	5 mL
½ tsp.	salt	2.5 mL
¾ cup	butter, softened slightly	180 mL
2 Tbsp.	cold water	30 mL

FILLING		
¼ cup	sugar	60 mL
½ tsp.	ground cinnamon	2.5 mL
	Pinch of ground cardamom	
	Pinch of ground cloves	
	Pinch of ground nutmeg	
¼ cup	butter	60 mL
3	Fuji apples, peeled, cored, ⅛-inch/ 3-mm thick slices	3

Yields 6 galettes, each 4 inches/10 cm in diameter

Sugar Pumpkin Crème Brûlée

1	small sugar pumpkin (2 lb./1 kg)	
2 cups	whipping cream	500 mL
1	vanilla bean	1
⅓ cup	sugar	80 mL
9	egg yolks	9
½ tsp.	ground cinnamon	2.5 mL
½ tsp.	ground ginger	2.5 mL
½ cup	sugar to caramelize	125 mL

Yields 6 ramekins or custard dishes, each 6 oz./175 mL

Every fall, we look forward to getting beautiful small sugar pumpkins from our friends the King family at Hazelmere organic farm. These are the best for making pumpkin desserts, as they have a sweet dense flesh that doesn't get watery and that purées very smoothly. Adding pumpkin and spices to the custard of the crème brûlée works very well, as the finished dessert is reminiscent of a pumpkin pie, but with a silky, creamy texture.

TO MAKE Preheat the oven to 325°F/160°C.

Cut pumpkin into quarters; remove and discard seeds. Place pumpkin in a roasting pan, skin side down. Cover the pan with aluminum foil, shiny side in, and bake until pumpkin is tender, about 1 hour. Remove from the oven and allow to cool a little, then scoop out the flesh; discard the skin.

Purée pumpkin flesh in a blender or food processor until very smooth. Measure out 1½ cups/375 mL of the purée and set aside for the recipe. (Any leftover purée can be frozen for use in another pumpkin dessert or soup.)

Heat whipping cream in a saucepan on medium heat to just under a simmer. Slice vanilla bean in half lengthwise, scrape out seeds, then add seeds and husk to cream.

While whipping cream is heating, whisk together sugar, egg yolks, cinnamon and ginger in a large stainless steel bowl. Carefully pour just a few spoonfuls of scalded cream into the yolk mixture to temper it. Gradually add the rest of the cream, all the while whisking gently so as not to create any foam on the surface. Add warm pumpkin purée and stir to incorporate evenly.

Strain custard through a sieve, using the back of a spoon to push purée through. Carefully pour strained custard into the ramekins (or custard dishes). If any bubbles form on top, pop them using the point of a knife.

Place the ramekins in a roasting pan and add enough boiling water to come halfway up the sides of the ramekins. Bake until custard sets, 30 to 40 minutes. Remove from the oven and allow to cool. Refrigerate to chill thoroughly. (Will keep refrigerated, covered well, for a day or two.)

Once the brûlées are well chilled, they are ready to be finished. Sprinkle sugar evenly on top of the custard in each ramekin and wipe the rim clean. Caramelize sugar either by using a propane or butane torch, or by placing the ramekins under the broiler until the sugar melts and is golden. Allow to cool and serve.

Caramelized Pear Tarts

PASTRY

¾ cup	flour	175 mL
¼ cup	cornmeal	60 mL
2 tsp.	sugar	10 mL
½ tsp.	salt	2.5 mL
¼ cup	butter	60 mL
2 Tbsp.	cold water	30 mL

FILLING

½ cup	sugar	125 mL
¼ cup	butter	60 mL
3	pears	3

Yields 6 tarts, each 4 inches/10 cm in diameter

A variation on the traditional Tarte Tatin made with apples, these individual pear tarts present beautifully at the dinner table. The pastry cups the natural shape of the pear and lifts the tart off the plate a little, giving a bit of height to the finished presentation and showing off the profile of the pear half, caramelized on top. We generally use Bartlett or Anjou pears, which are available from mid-September throughout the winter.

TO MAKE PASTRY Preheat the oven to 400°F/200°C.

Combine flour, cornmeal, sugar and salt in a bowl. Cut butter into small pieces and work into flour mixture until the texture becomes mealy. Add water and stir until just combined. Cover and allow to rest for 20 minutes.

Divide dough into 6 pieces and roll out on a lightly floured surface to form rounds 4 inches/10 cm in diameter.

FILLING Make caramel by combining sugar and butter in a saucepan on medium heat; cook until golden, 3 to 4 minutes. Pour 2 Tbsp./30 mL of caramel into each tart pan.

Peel, core and halve pears. Place a half pear, cored side down, on top of the caramel in each pan. Take a pastry round and place it on top of each half pear, pressing down around it to follow the shape of the fruit.

Bake in the oven until pastry is golden and pear is cooked through, about 20 minutes. Remove from the oven and allow to rest for 5 minutes.

To serve, invert tarts onto individual warmed plates.

Caramelized pear tarts >

Belgian Chocolate Soufflé with Crème Anglaise

4	egg yolks	4
3 Tbsp.	sugar	45 mL
1½ cups	whipping cream	375 mL
½ cup	milk	125 mL
1 tsp.	vanilla extract	5 mL

A soufflé is a dish that always impresses guests when you bring it out at the end of a meal, but, surprisingly, it is very easy to make. People say that a soufflé has to be made, baked and eaten quickly—and although the latter two are correct, a chocolate soufflé, because of its nature, can be prepared ahead in the afternoon, or even the day before, and baked later. The chocolate sets so quickly in the refrigerator that it traps all the air in the egg whites, so the batter cannot collapse while it sits. Simply take your soufflé directly from the fridge, put a parchment collar around it and bake in a preheated oven.

TO MAKE CRÈME ANGLAISE Place egg yolks and sugar in a bowl; whisk lightly until sugar is dissolved.

Combine whipping cream, milk and vanilla extract in a saucepan on medium heat; bring almost to the boiling point. Pour into the egg mixture a little at a time, whisking well. Pour back into the saucepan. Turn down the heat to medium-low; cook, uncovered, stirring constantly, until the mixture coats the back of a spoon, 3 to 4 minutes. Strain and cool. Refrigerate in a covered container until needed. (Will keep in the refrigerator for 2 to 3 days.)

TO MAKE SOUFFLÉS Butter the insides of the ramekins and dust with sugar. Refrigerate until needed.

Fill a medium saucepan with 2 inches/5 cm of water and bring to a boil. Turn off the heat but leave the pot on the burner. Combine chocolate and butter in a stainless steel bowl; place the bowl over the pan of hot water for mixture to melt. Whisk in egg yolks one at a time, and then liqueur, mixing well. Remove from the stove and set aside.

In another bowl, whisk together egg whites and cream of tartar until soft peaks form. Add sugar and continue to beat until stiff but not dry.

Add a third of the egg whites to the chocolate mixture and blend well. Fold the remaining egg whites into the chocolate mixture until just combined.

Ladle the chocolate mixture into the prepared ramekins. Cover with plastic wrap and refrigerate until needed (will keep up to 24 hours).

To bake, preheat the oven to 400°F/200°C. Place the ramekins on a baking sheet, and place the sheet in the centre of the oven. Bake until soufflés are puffed and set, 15 to 18 minutes.

Serve immediately, with crème anglaise in a small pitcher to pass around.

SOUFFLÉS

	Butter for greasing	
	Sugar for dusting	
6 oz.	semi-sweet chocolate	170 g
3 Tbsp.	butter	40 mL
4	egg yolks	4
2 Tbsp.	coffee liqueur	20 mL
4	egg whites	4
¼ tsp.	cream of tartar	1 mL
⅓ cup	sugar	80 mL

Yields 4 to 6 ramekins, each 4 oz./ 125 mL

Caramelized Apple Upside-down Ginger Cake

	Butter for greasing	
	Flour for dusting	
2 Tbsp.	butter, melted	30 mL
¼ cup	brown sugar	60 mL
3	apples, peeled and cored	3
¾ cup	water	175 mL
½ cup	molasses	125 mL
1 tsp.	baking soda	5 mL
2 cups	flour	500 mL
½ tsp.	salt	2.5 mL
1 tsp.	ground ginger	5 mL
1 tsp.	ground cinnamon	5 mL
	Pinch of ground nutmeg	
1 tsp.	baking powder	5 mL
⅔ cup	unsalted butter, at room temperature	150 mL
½ cup	brown sugar	125 mL
1	large egg	1
	Whipped cream or ice cream	

Yields 1 cake, 10 inches/25 cm in diameter

This dessert is perfect for a cold winter night. The caramelized apples that are baked underneath this moist, spicy ginger cake create a beautiful topping when inverted. The best apples to use are Fuji, Gala or Spartan. This cake is best served warm, fresh from the oven, with either a little whipped cream or vanilla ice cream to complement it.

TO MAKE Preheat the oven to 350°F/175°C.

Grease and dust with flour the sides of a 10-inch/25-cm springform pan. Line the bottom with parchment paper, then brush it with the melted butter and sprinkle with brown sugar.

Cut apples into eighths and arrange on the bottom of the pan.

Bring water to a boil in a saucepan on high heat, then remove from the burner and stir in molasses and baking soda. Allow to cool until lukewarm.

Combine flour, salt, ground ginger, cinnamon, nutmeg and baking powder in a bowl.

Cream together unsalted butter and brown sugar in an electric mixer at medium speed, for about 3 minutes. Add egg and mix well. Change mixer to low speed and slowly add the flour mixture, alternating with the molasses mixture. Stir together well, making sure the sides and bottom are mixed in.

Pour batter into the prepared pan and bake until a skewer pushed into the centre of the cake comes out clean, 45 to 50 minutes.

Remove from the oven and allow to cool. While cake is still slightly warm, invert and carefully remove it from the pan.

To serve, cut cake into wedges and serve with whipped cream (or ice cream).

Pecan and Maple Syrup Tart

This version of a southern classic, made Canadian with the addition of maple syrup, is neither too sweet nor too runny, as can be sometimes be the case with a pecan pie. This pie can be made the day before, as the filling benefits from a day in the refrigerator to help it set firmly.

TO MAKE PASTRY Combine flour, sugar and salt in a bowl. Add butter and mix until the texture becomes coarse and mealy. Add water and combine well. Mix until dough forms a ball, taking care not to overmix. Flatten dough into a disk and wrap in plastic wrap. Allow to rest for 30 minutes.

Preheat the oven to 350°F/175°C.

On a lightly floured surface, roll out pastry to form a round 12 inches/30 cm in diameter. Line a 10-inch/25-cm tart pan with the pastry, and use the back of the tines of a fork to press down around the edge. Line the bottom of the pastry with a piece of parchment paper and fill with dried beans. (The dried beans, which keep the bottom of the tart shell flat while baking, can be kept and reused for this purpose.) Bake until pastry just begins to colour around the edges and bottom looks set, about 20 minutes. Remove the dried beans and allow the pie shell to cool.

FILLING Arrange toasted pecans to cover the bottom of the pie shell evenly.

Whisk together sugar, maple syrup, eggs, vanilla extract and flour in a bowl. Pour gently over pecans.

Bake in the oven until slightly puffed and the centre just wiggles when the pan is tapped on the side, 30 to 40 minutes. Allow to cool completely, then cover and chill thoroughly in the refrigerator before serving.

To serve, cut into slices and place on plates. Garnish with whipped cream.

PASTRY

¾ cup	flour	175 mL
1 tsp.	sugar	5 mL
½ tsp.	salt	2.5 mL
6 Tbsp.	butter, softened	90 mL
1 Tbsp.	cold water	15 mL

FILLING

2 cups	pecans, toasted lightly	500 mL
1 cup	sugar	250 mL
1 cup	maple syrup	250 mL
3	eggs	3
2 tsp.	vanilla extract	10 mL
2 Tbsp.	flour	30 mL
	Whipped cream for garnish	

Yields 1 tart, 10 inches/25 cm in diameter

Chèvre Cheesecake with Dried Fruit in Apricot Brandy Syrup

1 cup	mixed dried fruit (apricots, cherries, figs, etc.)	250 mL
1 cup	water	250 mL
½ cup	sugar	125 mL
¼ cup	apricot brandy	60 mL
1	cinnamon stick	1
1	vanilla bean	1

CHEESECAKE

1 cup	sugar	250 mL
2 pkg.	cream cheese (each 8 oz./225 g)	2 pkg.
12 oz.	fresh soft goat cheese	350 g
5	eggs	5
1	lemon, zest and juice	1
3 Tbsp.	flour	45 mL

Yields 1 cake, 9 inches/23 cm in diameter

This cheesecake, made with fresh soft goat cheese and a hint of lemon, is sure to please. It is made without a bottom crust and baked in a hot water bath, which allows it to cook slowly without cracking, keeping it nice and creamy inside. Apricots are a natural choice to use for the dried fruit, but I am also partial to both cherries and figs in the mix.

TO MAKE FRUIT IN SYRUP If your mixed fruit includes larger dried fruits like peaches or apricots, slice them so that the pieces of fruit are of roughly equal size.

Combine water, sugar and apricot brandy in a saucepan; bring to a boil on medium heat. Add dried fruit and cinnamon stick. Cut vanilla bean in half lengthwise, scrape out seeds, then add seeds and husk. Turn down heat to low and simmer, uncovered, for 10 minutes. Remove from the stove, cover and steep for 30 minutes. Remove and discard vanilla husk and cinnamon stick. Cool and refrigerate in a covered container. (Will keep in the refrigerator for 2 or 3 weeks.)

TO MAKE CHEESECAKE Preheat the oven to 300°F/150°C.

Cream together sugar, cream cheese and goat cheese in an electric mixer. Beat in eggs one at a time, then add lemon zest, juice and flour.

Pour batter into a 9-inch/23-cm springform pan. Wrap a piece of aluminum foil around the bottom of the pan to prevent water from leaking in through the cracks in the pan while baking.

Place the springform pan in a roasting pan. Pour in boiling water to come halfway up the sides of the cake pan. Bake until cake just wiggles in the centre when the pan is tapped at the side, about 1 hour.

Remove from the oven and allow cake to cool in the pan of water. When water has cooled to room temperature, lift out the springform pan and remove the foil. Cover and chill thoroughly in the refrigerator for at least 2 hours before removing the sides of the pan.

To serve, use a hot knife to cut wedges of cheesecake. Place on plates and spoon fruit and syrup over top.

STOCKS

About Stocks

We use four basic types of stock in this book: chicken, fish, shellfish and vegetable—plus corn broth, a variation on vegetable stock. As I said in one of my previous cookbooks, stocks are like money in the bank—you should try to have some on hand just in case.

Please do not be intimidated by the thought of making and storing stocks; they really are simple. I think the biggest challenge for novice cooks is to first of all get that large soup pot filled with water and onto the stovetop. The rest is easy. After all, stock is just intensely flavoured water.

When it comes to freezing stocks, I like to use a tip that the well-known television cooking personality Graham Kerr gave me. Measure out the cooled stock and pour into a number of shallow reusable containers (not glass). Cover these containers with lids and then freeze. When they have frozen solid, unmold and label them with the type of stock, measurement and date. Store the frozen disks of stock in zippered plastic bags filed vertically in the freezer. Now you have your stocks neatly stored, and the containers are free to be used again. I also do the same thing with any sauces and stews that I wish to store.

Chicken Stock

20 oz.	chicken bones or 1 whole chicken carcass	600 g
1	medium onion, chopped	1
1	medium carrot, chopped	1
1	celery rib, chopped	1
2	sprigs fresh thyme	2
1	bay leaf	1
1	sprig fresh parsley	1
6	whole black peppercorns	6
8 cups	cold water	2 L

Yields 8 cups/2 L

Chicken stock is the type most called for in this book. It is also probably the most popular one in anyone's kitchen because it is fairly light, has good round flavours and is very versatile in that it can be used for lots of recipes.

The only choice is, do you want it to be light or dark? Light is perfect for making soups or for poaching vegetables and so on, and it is slightly easier to make than dark. Simply place all of the ingredients in a large soup pot, cover with cold water and simmer.

To make dark chicken stock, you must first roast the bones and vegetables in the oven at 450°F/230°C until they turn golden and become caramelized, about 30 minutes. Then transfer to a soup pot, cover with cold water and simmer. The extra step of roasting the ingredients gives the stock a darker colour and deeper flavour, making it more suitable for use in recipes such as brown sauces.

TO MAKE Place all the ingredients in a soup pot on medium-high heat and bring to a boil. Turn down the heat to low and simmer, uncovered, for 2 hours; skim off any foam from time to time.

Strain the stock and allow to cool. Refrigerate or freeze until needed.

Fish Stock

2 lb.	fresh fish bones	1 kg
1	medium carrot, chopped	1
1	celery rib, chopped	1
1	medium onion, chopped	1
8 cups	cold water	2 L
1 cup	dry white wine	250 mL
2	sprigs fresh parsley	2
2	sprigs fresh thyme	2
2	sprigs fresh tarragon	2
1	bay leaf	1
6	black peppercorns	6

Makes 8 cups/2 L

Fish stock is the easiest of all stocks to prepare because it requires such a short cooking time. For most fish stocks, use only white fish bones from such fish as halibut, sole, turbot or cod. The bones are light in colour but give really good flavour and tend to contain less oil.

The bones of fish that are rich in oil, such as salmon or trout, can also be used to make stock for lovely rich soups such as chowders or seafood stews.

TO MAKE Preheat the oven to 450°F/230°C. Place the fish bones in a roasting pan and bake in the oven until golden, about 20 minutes.

Transfer to a large soup pot and add all the other ingredients. Simmer, uncovered, on medium heat for 45 minutes. Skim off any foam from time to time.

Strain the stock through a sieve lined with cheesecloth and allow to cool. Refrigerate or freeze until needed.

Shellfish Stock

2 lb.	shrimp, prawn, crab or lobster shells	1 kg
12	cups cold water	3 L
1 cup	dry sherry	250 mL
2	carrots, peeled and thinly sliced	2
3	celery ribs, thinly sliced	3
2	large onions, thinly sliced	2
1	garlic clove	1
1	small bunch fresh parsley	1
3	sprigs fresh thyme	3

Makes 12 cups/3 L

Use shrimp, prawn, crab or lobster shells, separately or together. Lobster or shrimp shells, when roasted, also make a delicious stock for lobster bisque or a seafood risotto.

TO MAKE Preheat oven to 450°F/230°C.

Rinse the shells under running water and place them in a roasting pan. Bake in the oven until dry: roast shrimp and prawn shells for 20 minutes, lobster and crab shells for 40 minutes.

Transfer the shells to a soup pot and crush lightly with a meat hammer or rolling pin. Add all the remaining ingredients and bring to a boil on medium-high heat, then turn down the heat to

low. Simmer, uncovered, for 45 minutes. Skim off any foam from time to time.

Strain the stock through a sieve lined with cheesecloth and allow to cool. Refrigerate or freeze until needed.

Vegetable Stock

1	large onion, chopped	1
1	whole leek, thinly sliced	1
2	celery ribs, thinly sliced	2
2	carrots, thinly sliced	2
6	black peppercorns	6
1	bay leaf	1
1	sprig fresh thyme	1
2 cups	fresh parsley	500 mL
6	garlic cloves	6
1 Tbsp.	sea salt	15 mL
12	cups cold water	3 L

Makes 12 cups/3 L

Vegetable stock is a good substitute for chicken stock and can be used for soups, pasta, grain or rice dishes. It is also excellent for braising vegetables.

Make sure the vegetables are scrubbed well, but not peeled, and that any rotten parts are removed. If you do not, the stock may taste bitter. Gently roasting the vegetables caramelizes the natural sugars and gives more flavour to the stock.

TO MAKE Preheat oven to 450°F/230°C.

Place onion, leek, celery and carrots into a roasting pan and roast for 30 minutes.

Transfer to a soup pot and add all the other ingredients. Simmer, uncovered, on medium heat for 30 minutes. Skim off any foam from time to time.

Strain the stock and allow to cool. Refrigerate or freeze until needed.

Sweet Corn Broth

12	ears corn	12
1 cup	onion, 1-inch/ 2.5-cm cubes	250 mL
2 cups	carrot, 1-inch/ 2.5-cm cubes	500 mL
1	bay leaf	1
2	garlic cloves	2
2	sprigs fresh thyme	2
16	cups water	4 L

Makes 16 cups/4 L

This tasty corn broth can be used in place of vegetable stock. It uses cobs of corn after the kernels have been removed. The best time to make it is when you'll be using the corn kernels and corn broth in a recipe such as Sweet Corn and Celery Root Chowder (page 43) or Chanterelle and Sweet Corn Risotto (page 125), as there'll be broth left over.

TO MAKE Use a sharp knife to cut off the kernels from the corn (use corn kernels in a recipe). Cut cobs in half.

Place corncobs and all the other ingredients in a soup pot. Bring to a boil on medium-high, then turn down the heat to low and simmer, uncovered, for about 1 hour. (If you want a stronger flavour, simmer longer to reduce the broth even more.) Skim off any foam from time to time.

Strain the broth and allow to cool. Refrigerate or freeze until needed.